PR/

Behind the Curtain

"This book is a must-have reference for any new leader and for all those who are still behind the curtain—whether they are aware of it or not!"

—Carmen Sims, MBA, RN

"By blending personal experiences with real-world applications, Monica brings the reader on a journey of awareness into what is at the heart of leadership, showing how serving others is essential to success."

—Benjamin Dimas, RN, Area Vice President of Operations

"Monica combines professional leadership science with the personal vulnerability necessary for a true servant leader, making this book deeper than any I've ever encountered in leadership literature."

—Reverend Brice Higginbotham, a priest of the Diocese of Houma-Thibodaux

"As a Catholic priest, I have felt the uncomfortable pressure when asked to step into different leadership roles without always having the proper preparation and training. *Behind the Curtain* provided me with a concrete path to grow in servant leadership and helped me equip myself for future challenges. I've read a lot of leadership books, but none of them have helped transform me into a greater servant leader than this one!"

—Reverend Jacob Dumont, LC, Chaplain for Lumen Institute, New Orleans

"There is hope! Many aspiring leaders do not receive the proper modeling or tools they need as they move into advanced roles. For better or worse, they simply mimic previous *bosses* taking on bad habits and ineffective communication. Reading *Behind the Curtain* literally made me breathe a sigh of relief. Thanks to this book's transparency and practical tips, the reader can see a clear path to becoming the leader they've always wanted to be. Monica's gifts of openness and authenticity are inspiring, and she proves that it's never too late to course correct. So many will relate to the words she speaks and, more importantly, the world will be left a little bit better when readers choose to embrace and put into practice the gifts Monica is offering in this book."

—Kristi Fredieu, MBA, Director of Marketing and Business Development

"Monica's passion for developing leaders is evident in *Behind the Curtain*. She lets us see what happens behind the scenes—the highs and lows of leadership. Even after many years in leadership roles, it's clear that Monica understands the perspective and plight of frontline employees."

—Mechelle Roberthon, CPTD, MCCT, MS, MOS

"Spot on! It was real and resonated with me as a leader. I learned and rediscovered ideas to aid in my development. In today's world of healthcare, it can be hard to be objective. These things matter to me as a human on this planet."

—Agnes Broussard, RN, Support Supervisor for Coastal / Florida Division

"With vivid illustrations, Rougeau unveils her former façade and past fears, followed by her increased fidelity to God's call. Over time she becomes a better wife and mother, and to her surprise, she is transformed into a much more effective leader. As we listen to God's promptings and are led by the sound advice of others, we too can become more cheerful and enthusiastic servant leaders."

—Very Reverend Jared Suire, V.E., a priest of the Diocese of Lafayette

Behind the Curtain: Discovering the Servant Leader Within

By Monica Rougeau

First published in 2020 by

Monica Rougeau

www.elevareintl.com

First Edition

Editing + Proofreading by Cavalletti Communications, www.cavacom.biz

Cover Design by brandRUSSO

Author Photograph by C323 Photography

Typesetting by Chloe Barton

TABLE OF CONTENTS

This book is dedicated to my husband, D.D., my quietly constant companion. You always encourage me to do what makes me happy. For that, and for so much else, you have my heart—forever.

And to the late Brother Anthony Freeman, LC, my very first coaching client, who inspired a vision and kindled the fire of passion for what would become an intensely rewarding career. For your guidance and your intercession, you will forever have my gratitude.

Introduction

In 2014, I stepped away from a 28-year career in healthcare. It was time. The industry, which had once felt like a natural home for me, no longer felt like the right fit.

The ever-changing regulatory environment and payment restructuring combined with the growing trend of mergers and acquisitions was creating an environment of uncertainty and fear. Many in upper management jockeyed for positions to feel secure, and I wasn't comfortable with the manipulative corporate maneuvering. I was done playing the political games, and I needed to do something different—to make a very different kind of impact. I was convinced there was more to life (and to business) than this.

Late one evening, I came home from a particularly tough day at work. I walked in the front door and crumbled onto the floor of the foyer. When my husband walked in and saw me crying with my hands in my face, he simply gave me one of his patented knowing looks. This had become something of a pattern. The tears were new, but he had grown used to seeing me walk in at the end of the day completely deflated. He knew, though, that this was something different.

"I just don't want to do it anymore," I said.

"Then just quit!" he said.

"I can't quit" I shouted back at him. "I'm not a quitter!"

I thought about this and about my husband's advice as I got into bed that night, and I continued to think about it until I fell asleep. I envied his certainty. The solution seemed so obvious to him, but it couldn't be that simple, could it?

The next morning, I sprang out of bed with a new sense of purpose and determination. I drove to work, sat down at my desk, and began writing my letter of resignation.

My last day was in mid-September, and the changing of the seasons seemed appropriate. I decided that I would allow myself some time to decide what my next career move would be. I wanted to enjoy the holiday season with my family for once. My career and its constant pressures had always kept me from giving all of myself to my children and my husband, and I was determined to change this.

For the first 30 days, though, I allowed my body to dictate how I spent my time and, truth be told, I spent most of that month sleeping. I did not realize the level to which my career had depleted me. I would wake up in the morning, but I would stay in bed, my eyes closed. My body felt so heavy—like my limbs were glued to the mattress. When I was up and about, it was a struggle to even stand tall. My eyes were so heavy that I had to fight the urge to close them almost constantly. I wasn't thinking about much of anything during this time. It was a struggle to remain upright—let alone to spend time reflecting on my past or thinking about my future.

When the kids went back to school after the holidays, I finally found enough mental energy to spend some time reflecting on what I loved about work and what I hated about it. A big part of me missed the office, but it wasn't the corporate meetings I missed. It was the one-on-one time with the people on my teams. I had moved upward in the organization because I was very good at building teams and forming leaders. I was determined to forge a new path, determined to do something that would play into my passions and strengths.

I wanted to do something different, to disrupt the cycle, and to form new kinds of leaders—the kinds of leaders we need now more than ever. Not long after this, I founded Elevare.

Why Do We Need New Kinds of Leaders?

There is a mounting body of evidence that shows, first, how important leadership formation is in today's business climate and, second, the negative impacts that result when we forego this kind of training. The US Bureau of Labor recently found that companies with fewer than 100 employees give an average of only 12 minutes of management training every six months. This number is cut in half in larger organizations of 100 to 500 employees. This is not nearly enough.

Now, you might assume that this is because new leaders arrive to their positions armed with the knowledge they need to lead, but this is not the case. Researchers have found that up to 85% of new managers enter their roles without any kind of dedicated leadership training, mentoring, or coaching. They get a firm pat on the back, a *go get 'em, Tiger*, and nothing more. The results of this are clear: leaders who don't really know how to lead.

When leaders are ill-equipped to deal with the challenges of the modern workplace, the environment becomes toxic. Not only will the organization struggle to yield sustainable success, it will be plagued by unhappy and unfulfilled employees (not the most productive bunch). Communication is ineffective, morale is low, burnout is high, and there is high employee turnover. Rather than respecting their leaders, employees fear them. They worry about their job security, and they form cliques that make them even more difficult to manage.

Poor leadership is causing physical and mental strain. Poorly led workers frequently report problems like upset stomach, headaches, fatigue, and disturbed sleep patterns. They are more likely to be depressed, anxious, and frustrated. Their blood pressure is higher, they suffer more often from cardiovascular disease and weakened immune systems. Can we really expect these employees to give us their best?

Researchers from the Centers for Disease Control found that work stress is the leading workplace health problem and a major occupational health risk, ranking above physical inactivity and obesity. Stressful working conditions are associated with increased absenteeism and tardiness. What's more, healthcare expenditures are nearly 50% higher for workers in toxic workplaces. All of this combined is costing American businesses upwards of $36.4 billion every year.

In a 2019 study by the Society of Human Resource Management, researchers found that 58% of employees who quit a job due to workplace culture say that, ultimately, it was their relationship with management that led them to leave. There are certainly other factors to consider, but what we're looking at here is primarily a leadership issue. As leaders, we are failing our people.

The Benefits of Effective Leadership

When organizations put effective leadership development programs in place, they often see dramatic changes—some of them immediate, others emerging over time. A joint study by the Conference Board and Development Dimensions International found that when organizations put leadership development programs in place, they enjoyed the following benefits:

- Sales increased by 114%
- Productivity increased by 36%
- Employee turnover was 77% lower
- Operational efficiency improved by 42%

I've seen the truth of this from both sides (both as an employee and as a leader). I've seen how leadership training impacts an organization's bottom line while also producing more fulfilled and more successful employees (and managers).

Leadership training helped me better understand myself and the members of my team. It gave me a new appreciation for them, and that appreciation made me a better leader. As I grew my leadership abilities, I saw this growth reciprocated all around me. Team dynamics and productivity improved, and I could feel the stress levels dropping inside and all around me.

When I learned to become a better leader, I saw a change in the way members of my team responded to me and to each other. By being a better leader, I was helping create better employees and priming them to one day become better leaders themselves. Before this, I had unwittingly played a part in perpetuating the vicious cycle. I was the kind of boss nobody wanted, and I was creating poor employees who would go on to become tomorrow's poor leaders. When I learned how to lead, I found that I could, with a little effort, break the cycle.

With this book, I want to help you break the vicious cycle. By discovering the servant leader within, you'll be able to form the next generation of conscious and responsive leaders. By equipping ourselves, we'll be in a position to equip those we lead with the tools they need to better serve their teams and their organizations.

We start this journey with a look behind the curtain.

Behind the Curtain

In the classic film *The Wizard of Oz*, Dorothy's journey down the Yellow Brick Road culminates in an encounter with the Wizard. His voice booms at Dorothy and her companions.

Lightning flashes and smoke fills the room. The Wizard seems all-powerful, but then Dorothy's little terrier takes the curtain in his teeth and pulls it back, revealing the feeble old humbug working the machinery.

This memorable scene teaches us a powerful lesson about leadership. The people of Oz assumed that the Wizard had all the answers. They tolerated his (literally) explosive outbursts and his unreasonable demands because they believed he was all-knowing and all-powerful. They saw his authority as unassailable.

Behind the curtain, though, he was a man of flesh and blood. The minute that Toto pulled that curtain aside, the Wizard's seemingly supernatural authority evaporated. He had relied on bluster and pyrotechnics to create an illusion of power, but it was all smoke and mirrors. The minute the secret was out, he reverted to a more harmless and benevolent version of himself.

The Wizard may have been a liar, but he wasn't a bad man. He was just wrapped up in the story that others told about him. He used fear because he had tried it once and it had worked. He never stopped to ask himself whether he could have led any other way.

Leaders often find themselves in a similar situation. They are good people, but they get wrapped up in the stories that they tell themselves. When they are first promoted into a leadership position, they are more concerned with projecting leadership (i.e., strength, confidence, vision, etc.) than with being good leaders. It's simply easier to hide behind the curtain and play the role than it is to let those you lead see you for who you really are.

This is, at its heart, a problem with expectations. New leaders are expected to perform at a high level and produce results. They are often ill-prepared for the role's demands, and they know that there is someone waiting in the wings if they fail. They fall into the trap of projecting a particular (and toxic) brand of leadership. This produces a culture of distrust and smoke-and-mirrors leadership. Leaders and those they lead are both constantly looking over their shoulders, expecting to be replaced at any moment, and leaders do everything they can to conceal their inadequacies from those both above and below them. Both the leader and the led operate out of fear, neither realizing their true potential.

I've had the privilege of helping leaders in both the spiritual and the secular world develop their leadership abilities. I've spent years behind the curtain, watching leaders operate and seeing how freighted they are with expectations and how prone they are to self-doubt. We've placed them in the pressure-cooker of expectation and asked them to do things they are simply not equipped to do.

In the world of business, they are expected to know how to lead a team, when just the week before they were a part of that team. They knew next to nothing about what happens behind the curtain. The next thing they know, they are operating the machinery. I've seen the same thing with church leaders with whom I've worked. As a leader of his flock, a Catholic priest is expected to be above reproach. He is expected to know how to lead that flock, even if he has zero leadership experience. The organizations are very different, but their leaders face very similar challenges.

We need to prepare those new to leadership for the task ahead of them. We also need to help veteran leaders learn a few new tricks. We do this by helping them to become servant leaders.

Servant Leaders

Servant leaders either know instinctively or have been taught that their success as a leader is predicated on their ability to help their people succeed. This isn't just about giving them tasks they can execute effectively. It's much more than this. It's helping them define and then reach their ultimate level of success.

The servant leader leads through influence—not by command. They don't lead like Pontius Pilate; they lead like Jesus. They inspire others with their example and shape them with their words. They don't bark orders, they communicate vision. They breathe their spirit into their words, and those who follow them believe—believe with all their hearts—that they are doing, not just what is necessary, but also what is right.

The servant leader adapts his or her leadership style to suit the circumstances—the unique needs of the moment and of the people involved. This kind of flexible leadership ultimately addresses the foundational human needs of the led. It recognizes the importance of these needs and, by serving these needs, it allows for the organization and its constituent parts to flourish. Leaders and those they lead are both given the room to reach for self-actualization. When a team grasps self-actualization, the entire organization flourishes.

To what kind of needs do servant leaders tend? Let's start to answer that question with a look at Maslow's Hierarchy of Needs.

Conventional leaders try to leapfrog from the bottom of the pyramid to the top. They put money in their employees' pockets, allowing the employee to feed and clothe themselves and put a roof over their heads, but this only covers their physiological needs. Our true satisfaction runs deeper than this. We also need safety, and, deeper still, we have psychological needs that must be filled if we are to realize our potential.

Authoritarian leaders leave these needs entirely unaddressed, and then they wonder why their employees can't reach their full potential. The answer is staring them in the face: they're trying to put a capstone on an unfinished pyramid.

Are you providing a safe work environment? This means more than following OSHA guidelines. It also includes making sure that, when employees have ideas or concerns, they feel safe in bringing these to their supervisor—without fear of ridicule or retribution.

Are you providing for their psychological needs? Are you forming and leading complementary and cohesive teams? Are you recognizing their strengths and acknowledging their accomplishments? Are you providing opportunities for them to hone existing skills and develop new ones?

Finally, are you empowering them? Are you fully equipping them to stand on their own two feet? Are you priming them to reach new levels of success that may not include you?

Few leaders can answer *yes* to any of these questions (let alone all of them). Those who can answer *yes* are the servant leaders, and they are primed for this new decade and the challenges it will bring.

Servant leaders might not have all the answers, but they don't present themselves as all-knowing. They might not be able to accomplish everything they set their mind to, but they don't present themselves as all-powerful. Their teams believe in them. They've built up deep reserves of faith and confidence. They're fallible humans leading other fallible humans. With the help of those they lead, though, they can move mountains.

If you are tired of being exhausted, overwhelmed, frustrated or stuck, take this journey with me. Become a servant leader. Lead yourself and others out of the chaos and into the calm. The right approach to leadership will help you discover (or re-discover) the joy of your vocation. It will help you shine more brightly so that you can lead the way for others. As a servant leader, you'll be helping mold tomorrow's servant leaders. You'll be serving them—and serving the future generations they will one day lead themselves.

1

The Lion's Den

"I will prepare and some day my chance will come."

—Abraham Lincoln

The Romans loved spectacle. In the second century AD, they punished criminals publicly and gruesomely. The worst of these punishments was *damnatio ad bestias* "condemnation to the beasts." Christians and runaway slaves (the two worst forms of criminal in the Roman world) would have wild beasts set upon them while the Colosseum's spectators roared with delight. They were literally thrown to the lions.

Untold numbers of Christians lost their lives in these grisly spectacles. In their last moments, many of them must have hoped that God would protect them in the same way he had protected Daniel when King Darius of Babylon had thrown him into the lion's den centuries earlier. There are stories of miraculous survival, but the lion's share didn't live to tell the tale.

Today, we say that someone is "thrown to the lions" if they are handed a task that is out of their depth. We no longer literally feed criminals to the lions, but we do, metaphorically, feed new leaders to the lions every day. We place individuals in leadership positions before they are equipped to handle the challenges they will soon face. We expect them to fend for themselves.

Daniel needed divine intervention to survive his night in the lion's den. We can't count on this kind of intercession. Those who are elevated to leadership positions likely won't be saved from the lion's jaws by a heavenly host. They'll sink or swim based on their leadership abilities.

What might happen if we were to prepare and protect new leaders with training and ongoing guidance? What might happen if we arm them and shield them before they come face to face with the lions?

Why New Leaders Fail

When leaders fail, it is often because we have not prepared them to face the lions. They are cast into the pit in their birthday suit. They're given no sword or shield, and, worst of all, no lifeline (no way to haul themselves out of the pit and regroup). We aren't developing them or offering them ongoing guidance. Expectations come at them from every angle—from peers, superiors, and from within themselves. They either survive by the skin of their teeth or their bones are picked clean. More often than not, they are chewed up and spit out. They might survive, but the experience scars them. They crawl out of the pit missing an eye, an ear, or perhaps a limb. They end up less effective as leaders, and they often end up presiding over and contributing to toxic cultures.

Imagine for a moment that you've been promoted into a senior leadership position. Initially, you may feel proud and deeply grateful for the opportunity. Someone has recognized something in you—perhaps your abilities or perhaps your work ethic. These positive feelings are short lived, though. The moment you step into this new role, it all falls on you like a ton of bricks. There are new programs and processes to learn, new responsibilities, new people to report to, and new people who are reporting to you. From above and below come questions that you're expected to answer. How would you react in this situation?

Most new leaders try to throw energy at the problem by working longer hours and giving more of themselves to the role, but this can only last for so long. Exhaustion eventually catches up with them. They try to manage the snowballing stress that increased expectation brings with it, but this too has its breaking point. They crack under the pressure and end up frustrated and resentful. Without any tangible support or resources, they withdraw further and further into isolation.

They either sit back and play passive, waiting for people to get used to them before they make any changes, or they try to start a revolution. They either don't change enough, or they change too much. Both of these approaches often produce inconsistent results. Change can't be avoided, but at the same time it can't be forced. You can't sit back and wait for the lions to fall asleep, but you also can't leap straight from the lip of the pit onto the back of the biggest lion and start riding for all you're worth.

Some (usually those with some form of leadership training and support) find a way out of the lion's den. Some manage to find a way to lull the lions to sleep without any training or support. These leadership rock stars, the bright, enthusiastic, and ambitious newbies who are keen to grow both professionally and personally, have God-given leadership gifts, but a large organization will be lucky if it has one or two of these.

The vast majority of effective leaders *learn* how to lead. Just as the weightlifter doesn't go from lifting ten pounds to throwing 100 pounds over his head in one snatch, the effective leader learns before leading. They work up to it. To rise to the challenge, leaders must (like the bodybuilder) build muscle.

What are you doing to build your leadership muscles? How are you preparing for that day when you leap (or are thrown) into the pit?

Advancement Without Growth

If you're not doing enough (or anything) to develop your leadership muscles, you'll be falling into a cycle that traps countless executives: advancement without growth.

I spent decades trapped in this cycle. I was an ambitious and eager young woman when I entered the corporate homecare field in the mid-nineties. I started at an entry-level clerical position, but I rose quickly through the ranks. Within five years, I was the Chief Operating Officer of a state-wide company. Two years later, I held two titles: COO and CFO.

This rapid advancement satisfied my ambitious side, but something was missing. I didn't know what it was then, but I do now. I was advancing, but I wasn't growing.

I was scaling the corporate ladder, but my advancement came with little training, support, or resources. I was gaining knowledge day by day, but I lacked the wisdom I needed to be an effective leader. There was no environment in which I could sharpen my leadership skills, no safe space of support and encouragement in which I could make mistakes and learn from them, no ability to explore ways that my leadership and my values could be brought into alignment.

I had been thrown to the lions, and I had managed to survive, but only just barely.

With every advancement, I dug myself in further and further. I did everything I needed to survive, but nothing that would help me thrive. Each night, when I got home, I nursed my wounds and self-medicated. I worked longer and longer hours, slept less and less, and I relied on unhealthy coping mechanisms: alcohol, food, and over-the-counter medications. Rather than reflecting for even a moment on what I was doing and where I was going, I zoned out on the couch every night. This was the only way I could get from one day to the next.

I no longer recognized myself when I looked in the mirror. Stress had changed me. I was overweight and overwhelmed. I hadn't slept a solid seven or eight hours in what felt like years. I was constantly on edge, constantly looking over my shoulder.

Each time I thought I had crawled out of the lion's den, I found myself flat on my back surrounded by snarling faces. I fought back with everything I had. I had an image in my mind of what a leader was, and I was trying as hard as I could to be this kind of leader. I tried to control those beneath me, and I acted like a dictator when challenged. This was, I thought, what leaders did. This is how I'd been led, and it had been (in its way) effective, so I became the hypocrite—becoming the kind of leader I had once criticized.

When I was at the beginning of my career, I had been told (more times than I can count) that I needed to toughen up. I needed to develop a thick skin if I was going to make it as a leader in this industry, so that's what I did. With each advancement, I added a new layer of armor.

Inside that armor, I was as small and afraid as I had been on the day I started. I had advanced, but I had not grown. If anything, behind the curtain I had placed between me and my team, I had shrunk. Members of my team never saw my authentic self. I never let myself appear vulnerable in front of them. My personal and professional lives were completely compartmentalized.

Focused on doing and being the perfect executive, I worked longer and harder than anyone else. I was (as far as my employees knew) composed, non-emotional, and focused on getting the job done. The organization was growing, and my team was performing in line with expectations. That (I thought) was enough. My personal growth would have to wait.

Seeing Through New Eyes

As we entered this new century, the organization I was working for was growing, and the industry was changing around us. We began to encounter challenges with staff turnover and recruitment, so we decided to try an employee engagement survey. I thought I was prepared for what the survey would tell us, but I wasn't.

The colleague who brought me the results looked as though he had drawn the short straw and had to be the one who told me that my dog had just been run over.

"Monica," he said, "the results from the employee engagement survey are in."

"Ok, what does it say?"

"The staff don't like you."

"What do you mean they don't like me?"

"They call you 'the ice *itch'."

It felt like he'd punched me in the gut. I retreated into my office, closed the door, and tried to catch my breath. I sat in there in the dark for quite some time. I stared at my bookcase and asked myself some difficult questions: How did I get here? How did I become *that* kind of leader, that toxic bully?

My eyes came to rest on the spine of one of my books, *Becoming a Person of Influence* by John Maxwell. I went to the shelf and picked it up and thumbed its pages. I had read it years earlier, but now I was seeing it through different eyes. As a young leader, I had read this book (and many of the books next to it on the shelf) because that's what I was *supposed to do.* I didn't absorb the content or apply the principles. I had gone through the motions by turning the pages, but I had closed the book no wiser than when I had opened it.

Something had changed, though. I was questioning what I thought I knew. For the first time, I could see how wide the gap was between the kind of leader Maxwell was describing and the kind of leader I was. It was with this realization that my life and career began to change.

Autocratic Leadership

Without fully realizing it, I had become an autocratic leader. When I first entered the workforce, this was the dominant leadership style. Its appeal is a result of its simplicity. Power is placed in the hands of one person, who then decides what everybody will do and how they will do it. The team is essentially an afterthought. They have very little trust and even less freedom.

During times of upheaval, autocratic forms of leadership might become expedient or even necessary. When pivoting or re-organizing, you need a strong hand on the tiller, but this should only ever be a temporary solution. When it becomes a long-term or permanent leadership strategy, problems arise.

Organizations that continue to practice authoritarian micromanagement are diminishing their potential. Considering the rapidly changing leadership climate, they may even be working their way out of existence. Today's most desirable employees have more options than ever before. If they feel they're being managed autocratically, or if they feel like the organization they work for is out of alignment with their deeply held values, they'll run for the exits as fast as their legs will take them.

These employees are not expendable. They are a finite resource, and they need to be led in a way that makes them feel valued and supported. Autocratic leaders see their people as disposable and replaceable. When the organization hits a rough patch, they cut a swathe through the office, letting people go left and right.

This is entirely the wrong approach. A former CEO once told me, "You cannot cut your way to prosperity. You have to grow!" The autocratic leader constantly asks his people to do more with less. Their first solution is to cut physical resources, shortly followed by cutting their people (human resources). The servant leader gives his or her people what they need to grow.

PAST	PRESENT	FUTURE
Oversees Compliance	Oversees Performance	Oversees Potential
Focused On Correction	Focused On Improvement	Focused On Possibility
Looks Over The Shoulder	Looks Over The Results	Looks Over Alignment
Enforces Policy	Enforces Productivity	Enforces Purpose
Demands Subordination	Demands Cooperation	Demands Innovation

We're seeing more and more each day that this kind of people-centered approach is the way forward. The days of the autocratic leader are behind us. Ahead, we can look forward to the rise of the servant leader. We turn the page the moment we start recognizing what is behind leadership failures.

We are witnessing a dramatic change in effective leadership styles—driven largely by changing expectations from employees. We are entering the new age of the servant leader, and the organizations that are getting ahead of the curve will be the ones that are best prepared for the challenges ahead.

Sword and Shield

Nobody wakes up in the morning and says, "Today, I will be a terrible leader." Leaders do the best they can with the available tools. When we add effective tools to the leader's toolbox, we equip them for success. Rather than facing the wild beasts unarmed, leaders equipped in this way are fortified with sword and shield. They're prepared to face down even the toughest lions.

Here's the thing, though. Leaders need to be convinced to arm themselves. Many of them are convinced that they can do it on their own without help. They've found a way to survive in the lion's den. Convincing them that there is a better way isn't exactly easy.

Change is uncomfortable. People generally only change when the pain of staying the same is greater than the pain of change. This means we end up waiting until we are at our wits' end to see that our approach to leadership isn't working. We change only when we have to, and our organizations and teams suffer in the meantime. We need to get better at recognizing the problems caused by poor leadership, and we need to be prepared to act on these issues well before they get out of hand and force us to act.

When leaders are armed with the right leadership strategies and shielded with the right problem-solving approaches, they'll be able to plant their feet in the ground. The lions may roar and paw the ground, but the leader is prepared.

Rather than reacting, they are planning and anticipating difficulties. This means that they can prepare their teams for the road ahead. The goal is clear, and so is the direction.

2

Stop the Madness

"Bad leaders believe that they have to project control at all times."

—Simon Sinek

When I was in my early thirties, I looked and felt like someone much older. I was overweight from a combination of stress-eating and poor diet. I was travelling for work so much that I would often go weeks between home-cooked meals. No matter how much sleep I got, I always looked tired.

I hated the way I looked, but I was convinced I could turn this all around with a fancy outfit or makeover. I wore expensive suits and heels, and I got my hair, makeup, and nails done every time I felt like I needed a pick-me-up (which was almost always).

When I was feeling extra fluffy, I would find anything that made me feel better, even if only for a moment. I would head to the department store for a quick stress shopping spree. I would pile clothes high on the counter and slap down the plastic. I would tell myself I deserved it. The pleasure I felt at the point of purchase rarely lasted; by the time I got home, I felt just as bad—

sometimes worse. Most of the outfits I purchased found their way to the back of the closet, never to be seen again.

I had managed to convince myself that new clothes would give me that boost of confidence I was lacking and make me look like the woman I wanted to feel like, but these impulse purchases did nothing for my confidence. My husband and I were both earning very comfortable incomes at this time, so I wasn't putting our financial health in jeopardy. Still, I knew I was spending frivolously, and I felt guilty every time I looked at my credit card statements. I was not transparent with my husband about some of my purchases (a slippery slope if there ever was one), and although he never asked how much I had spent or whether I really *needed* what I had bought, I would often try to rationalize my purchases to him. I'd tell him that this item or that one had been on sale. He allowed me to justify my behavior (to both of us) in this way.

And this was just the tip of the iceberg. I was working so much and so hard that, when our paths did cross, it was for the briefest of moments. We occasionally sat side by side on the couch at the end of the evening, but my thoughts were always elsewhere. All I talked about was work, and I spent more time talking about my colleagues (many of them male) than I did asking my husband about his day. He seldom said very much; he mostly sat there and listened.

Years later, reflecting on that time, I realized how hurtful that had to have been for him. The majority of my attention and emotional energy was being given to others. He felt that he did not belong in my world. Indeed, at times he questioned whether he even belonged in my life. I didn't show him how important he was to me. Quite the opposite, I pushed him further and further away. He didn't feel needed. He didn't see a place for himself in my career-oriented world. It's a testament to his faith and fidelity that he stayed with me through this period.

My Children Deserved More than My Leftovers

My husband wasn't the only one who was getting less of me than he deserved. My children only got my leftovers while I was climbing the corporate ladder. My leadership style was all about control, and that meant I had to constantly feed energy into the system. I needed work, and I wanted my team to need me—to depend on me for leadership. By micro-managing and second-guessing my team, I created this kind of dependent culture. Nothing could happen without my input. This was, I thought, what leadership meant, and I willingly sacrificed my time and energy to keep what I had built from crumbling. I didn't cordon off any time for me or for my family. The job took everything. Whenever there was a problem (i.e., almost constantly), I took yet more time and energy away from my family and fed it into the system.

Throughout all these years, I would often work on weekends, and this would mean bringing my daughter to work with me. She was eager to help (bless her heart), so I would put her to work sorting scrap paper or, as she got a little older, making labels and doing data entry and records maintenance. I would get lost in my work, and this would mean my daughter and I would both put in a full day. We'd go home exhausted—hardly model parenting.

I regret it to this day that, for years, I only gave my children and my husband my leftovers. I let my career consume me, and, as so often happens, its hunger was insatiable. It wasn't satisfied with just me. It just kept feeding, consuming my family life and social life, and it still wanted more.

After years of this, I found myself on an island of success. Passing all around me was the current of life. I was always too busy to participate in social functions, and friends drifted away. I told myself that nobody understood what I was going through. I didn't reach out to friends or family for support. I kept it all to myself, convinced that it was just another problem that only I could solve.

There were external stressors at work, but the vast majority of my stress was unknowingly self-driven. I was suffering from impostor syndrome. Because I had, at best, only a partial understanding of how to lead, I had the constant insecurity of not being good enough. I concealed these fears and inadequacies behind a constant flurry of activity. If I could just keep my hands busy, nobody would be able to see them shaking.

It was a recipe for isolation, and I was only making it worse by removing myself from the support system of my family and friends. I was spiraling into a pit of madness, and I was pulling my team with me. I pushed myself to the breaking point, and I would exert my authority and control over members of my team whenever I was feeling the pressure either from above or from within myself. I was a textbook autocratic leader.

Of course, I couldn't see this yet. I hated having autocratic bosses, and I was quick to criticize their dictatorial decision-making.

I had adopted the same leadership style, but I thought I was somehow different because my heart was in the right place. I could still criticize autocratic bosses because I didn't yet see how they and I were doing the same things for the same reasons. The flaws we are quickest to criticize in others are, more often than not, identical to our own. I would have seen this clearly if I would have allowed myself to see through someone else's eyes.

I wanted to do right by others. I wanted to be an exemplary leader, but I didn't know how to be anything other than an autocratic leader. With no awareness and no understanding, what else could I do but make the same mistakes over and over again?

If we want to break this cycle, we have to start with ourselves—with a recognition that we're not being the kinds of leaders we would want to follow.

3

What Does it Mean to be a Leader?

"The more you know about the past,
the better prepared you are for the future."

—Theodore Roosevelt

Several years ago, while conducting a series of international leadership workshops in Italy, one of our translators approached me with a problem. There was, he told me, no direct French or Spanish translation for the word *leadership.*

I was skeptical, so I did a little investigating, and what I found surprised me. There is no Latin or Greek derivation for the word *leadership.* The word comes, not from Latin or Greek but, rather, from the Old English word *lædan*, which means to guide or bring forth, and from its close Indo-European Germanic relative *laidjan, which means* to travel.

Travel, like leadership, is simply a movement from one place to another. Think of caravans in the old West or of Moses in the desert. The leader's job was to keep the group intact—to make sure that everybody arrived at the same destination. Even when the journey is long and the destination unclear, the effective leader keeps his people together.

We've forgotten what it means to be truly responsible to and for our people. To go forward, we need to go back—back to these earlier forms of leadership. We need to ask ourselves what it truly means to lead people. Only when we know what real leadership looks like and why it is important, will we be able to talk about effective ways to create tomorrow's leaders.

Tomorrow's truly effective leaders will be less concerned with key performance indicators (KPIs) than they will be with providing employees the opportunity to grow both as professionals and individuals. They'll lead with their heart, not just their head.

I used to lead with my head. I would be tasked with lifting the performance of an underperforming division, and I'd immediately apply logical formulas. I'd use KPIs as a benchmark, and I often found that things had to get worse before they got better. Those who weren't hitting their targets often left of their own accord, and those who just barely made it across the line felt stressed and uncertain about their future.

Undeniably, this is easier, and it produces short-term results, but at what cost? What kind of message does leading with metrics as the sole guide send to our teams? Does it serve them?

Servant Leadership: The Fellow Traveler

The servant leader, rather than commanding, sees himself or herself as a companion in a journey—a fellow traveler rather than a cattle driver. They want to help those they lead bring forth their full potential, while simultaneously realizing their own potential as leaders.

Servant leadership is not a quantifiable leadership style. The style of servant leaders varies from person to person, changing according to our unique flavors, strengths, temperaments and passions. Servant leaders, however, do share something in common: they are the helpers. They see potential in everybody, and they want to help bring what has been latent to the surface. They see themselves as successes or failures based on their ability or inability to do this.

Servant leaders guide others by helping those they lead grow and excel in ways suited to their talents and preferences. If, as an organization, we're all pulling at the same rope, the servant leader does more than just point at the rope and tell his people to pull. They find the right place for everyone so each member of the team can pull with all his or her might and make a difference. Whenever necessary, they knot the rope to give leverage to those they are asking to pull.

The servant leader fulfills all the necessary roles that keeps the caravan moving forward. At times they are leading from the front, providing the guiding light when the clouds roll in and hide the moon and the stars. At the head of the vanguard, they can clear the way and help those they lead spot and avoid the obstacles in their path.

At other times, they lead from behind. They provide support to those who have lost step with the rest of the group, encouraging and lifting rather than cracking the whip. This is how they ensure that the travelling party arrives intact at its destination.

And sometimes they lead from the middle. They walk side by side with those they lead, providing fellowship and camaraderie. They are keen to collaborate, and their doors (and ears) are always open. They provide a sounding board so that those they lead can debrief and reflect on experiences, and they act as a mentor, helping others gain first wisdom and then confidence.

Acting vs. Being

Being a servant leader is not just a role you play; it is an expression of your deepest self, of your authentic character. When your team is facing challenges, that is not the time to play a part and speak your lines. That is the time to search your heart and see what kind of leader you want to be. If you are receptive to what your heart tells you, the leader you are deep down will emerge. You (and your team) will see what you're really made of. If you play the role (even if you play the role of the servant leader), it will strike a false note. Rather than seeing your deep, authentic self, your people will see you as an actor—a counterfeit.

You can say the things that servant leaders say until the cows come home, but, if deep down you believe that you are better than those you lead, you are a fraud. If you hold yourself up as the model of a more sensitive form of leadership while, at the same time, you demand that people do things the way you want without question, you are a counterfeit servant leader.

If you say that you are putting your people first, you need to follow this up with something tangible. You should be spending the majority of your time working with your people to help them translate their efforts into results. You cannot lead from behind a desk. If you spend more time analyzing data than you do getting behind the numbers to talk to the people themselves, your priorities revolve around metrics, not people.

If you are going to talk like a servant leader, you'll need to act like one too.

What Are Your People Getting from You?

During my last years in healthcare, I spent a considerable amount of my time doing what I loved to do: forming leaders. I worked with a core group of leaders, each of them responsible for their own agency, and I also worked with those who were clearly destined for leadership roles, helping develop them and train them to one day lead their peers.

Not a day went by without me having some kind of substantive, one-on-one interactions with at least one of these current or future leaders. I would meet with them in groups, talk to them over the phone, or, best of all, sit down behind closed doors to talk through things. When I wasn't working with them, I was thinking about how I could better serve them. I spent much of my time researching, trying to find solutions to their unique problems and ways to make them better leaders.

When I think of this time, I often find myself thinking of Wendy. She taught me a great deal about the power of investing time in people and about how we can be a companion for future leaders on their journey of growth.

I first met Wendy when I was tasked with rehabbing a struggling agency. My first order of business was meeting with a cross-section of agency staff, and Wendy was one of these. She had a large office, but it felt cramped. Her desk was covered with files piled in stacks that looked like they might topple at any moment. When I walked in, all I could see was the top of her head as she bent over the keyboard. The only sound was the clacking of the keys. She was typing away at a frantic speed.

I asked if I could have a moment of her time, and when she looked up, I could see there was real terror in her eyes. I tried to put her mind at rest by explaining that we would just be having a get-to-know-each-other chat. It was nothing formal. She seemed to relax a little, but I could see that she remained suspicious.

I asked her to tell me about her time with the company, and she told me she had been with the organization for five years. All that time, she had been a transcriptionist. She could process files faster than anybody else in her department (indeed, faster than anybody else I'd ever seen), so it made sense for the organization to leave her where she was. A small and skittish woman buried behind piles of paper, Wendy didn't complain. She just continued to plug away, quietly doing exactly what was asked of her. I asked her if she had ever been given the opportunity to try something else, or if she'd ever been encouraged to try something else she might be good at. She shook her head.

This was a problem. I knew that looming new requirements for electronic health records would result in new software being adopted by our organization. This would make Wendy and her skills obsolete, and I felt a sense of urgency. If Wendy didn't develop new skills, she would soon find herself out of a job. I wanted to help. If we could work together on growing her skills and her confidence, she'd be better positioned for the future. Even if she didn't stay with the company long term, she'd have the kind of transferrable skills that would make it easier for her to find rewarding employment elsewhere.

I told Wendy that, each week, we would spend one hour together working on developing new skills. We'd work with her existing strengths, but we'd try to add new skills as well.

She had doubts. Once again, I could see anxiety and fear in her eyes. She had spent so long doing one thing and doing it very well that she couldn't really imagine herself doing anything else, but this changed when we started to work together. As the weeks went by, she mastered new tasks, gaining confidence every day.

After a few months together, she had more than proved herself, so I recommended a transfer for her. A management position had opened up at one of the other offices. This not only meant a better opportunity and increased compensation for her; it also meant more time with her children. She was a single mother of two, and she had been commuting 45 minutes to and from work every day. The other office was only a few minutes' drive from her home.

She was nervous about the change, but I told her that the move would be a good one for her in every way, and I *knew* this to be true. She trusted me enough to apply for the position, and she flourished in her new role.

When I left the organization, Wendy was confidently and competently functioning as the office manager. Only a few months earlier, she had told me that she couldn't see herself doing anything other than the transcription work she had been doing for the past five years.

The work I did with Wendy was one of the things I reflected on when I was thinking about what I wanted to do with my life after leaving the healthcare industry. I could see that, by taking time to get to know Wendy and helping her develop her skills, I had helped both her and the organization. I treated Wendy, not as a cog in the machine but, rather, as a crucial contributor, a precious asset.

Through her, I started to understand what kind of leader I wanted to be, and what kind of leader I wanted to help other people become.

The Courage to Serve

When I first describe servant leadership to my clients, some respond with skepticism. Their reflex response is that the kind of leaders I am describing are soft. These kinds of warm and fuzzy leaders, the skeptics say, are pushovers. They don't get any respect.

I often respond by asking them what kind of leader does get respect. These same doubters tell me that leaders need to *command* respect. They need to exert their authority constantly. They need to let their people know who is in charge. This, they say, is what courageous leadership looks like. They have the courage to be disliked—this is what it takes to get stuff done.

Nothing could be further from the truth. The servant leader is the very definition of courageous leadership. Standing firm and doing what is right for the people you serve takes much more courage than hiding behind the veil of authority.

Franklin Roosevelt said, "Courage is not the absence of fear, but rather the assessment that something else is more important than fear." For the servant leader, that something else is the wellbeing of those they serve. There will be times when the decisions we must make leave us with uncertainty and fear, but the servant leader can push through this. They can face uncertainty with courage (and so can those they lead) because they know that, whatever comes, they will continue to do what's best for their teams.

Brave leaders are aware of their fears. They aren't fearless, even though they act fearlessly. Especially when you are starting to align yourself with the servant leader's path, you might feel doubts or fears. This is just old insecurities trying to re-establish themselves. Keep the faith. Keep doing what you know is right, and your fears will fade. They'll never disappear entirely, but you'll become better at recognizing them for what they are. Each time you do the right thing despite your fears or doubts, your confidence will grow and so will your momentum.

4

Beginning the Transformation

"Unless there's a personal transformation,
there can be no social transformation."

—Deepak Chopra

When we talk about personal transformation, too often we bring to it the idea that we need to become an entirely different kind of person. This is entirely the wrong idea. Transformation (even radical transformation) does not demand that we discard old identities in favor of entirely new ones. It simply means that we take a new shape.

We are the same material, but we have formed it into something new. We have retained the essence of who we are. We haven't started over from scratch; we've grown into better versions of ourselves, realizing the potential that was always there.

To do this, we need to first become cognizant of the fact that change is necessary. This awareness is the catalyst of change. We can't even begin to move toward something better until we recognize that better is possible. Indeed, we need to do more than this. We also need to recognize that better is *necessary.*

We don't know what we don't know, but we can't continue to use this as an excuse. We can't continue to go about our lives in our own little world, never looking up to see what we might be missing. Something has to come along and grab our attention and bring our awareness to the problem.

It might be some honest feedback from a boss or peer, it might be a book (maybe even this one), or it might be something you hear at a conference. It might be the birth of your first child, a brush with death, or a life-changing loss. Whatever it is, this awareness is an opportunity. Don't waste it.

If you're waiting for an epiphany or some kind of life-changing event to come along and force a change, let these words be that moment: you can be better. Unless you're already leading with a servant's heart, you *must* be better.

Getting Through a Thick Skull

I've said it many times: I am a stubborn woman. It seems that God has had to knock me over the head (sometimes more than once) to get my attention. When I was bossing rather than leading, I couldn't really see what I was doing. I was deep in the weeds, and I couldn't get above them to see the larger picture. Rather than trying to rise above, I dug down deeper.

The walls I placed around me grew thicker and thicker with each passing day. I was so obsessed with being respected that I closed my eyes entirely to the glaringly obvious. I was failing at home and at work, and I couldn't see it. I was the Great Wizard of Oz, working the gears and levers behind the curtain as hard as I could without once stopping to ask myself what kind of impact I was making.

I was always connected to work. I never turned off my phone or took vacation or sick days unless I was physically unable to get out of bed. On the few days I was too sick to make it to the office, I sat up in bed surrounded by an ever-growing mountain of tissues and worked on my laptop.

I remember looking back at an entire decade and recognizing that the only time I had taken off *in ten years* had been to give birth to my children. I could barely remember the last time I had taken a vacation with my family. I had travelled, but only ever for work. I would leave some of the places I visited saying that I would *love* to take my husband and children there someday, but these were empty words.

Year after year, I let vacation days lapse rather than using them. When I told the HR director that I'd rather continue working than take the vacation days I was entitled to, she gasped in horror. I took this as a badge of honor. My commitment was absolute. I was a company lady through and through. This was, I thought, what commitment looked like.

My husband and I hardly spent any time together. I had my career and he had his, and he had elderly parents who needed his help. Our rivers flowed in separate channels for years. I was so tightly wound that, at home and at work, I felt I could snap at any moment.

Still, I carried on, refusing to slow down. The idea of taking a break would make me curl my lips in disgust. Deep down, I knew that I was placing a tremendous strain on my marriage and on the relationship between me and my children, but it was much easier to ignore the problem than to face it.

I lost sight of what was truly important, and I'll never fully live this down. To this day, I'm still working on repairing the damage I did during those years.

Taking a Moment to Take a Moment

I was starting to become aware that I had a problem. I felt the growing strain in my personal life, and, at work, I was starting to see glimmers of the truth—that my autocratic, always-on leadership style was creating more problems than it was solving.

I decided that I would take a break. I was determined to take my children to the happiest place on earth, Disney World, so I started making plans to take the kids and my parents to the Sunshine State. My mom and I agreed that the trip would be a great experience for the kids, but it would also be a much-needed chance for me to unplug for a few days.

The plan was to drive to Orlando, and when I arrived to pick up my parents, before we even got in the car, my mom demanded that I give her my phone. I reluctantly handed it over. She turned it off and locked it in the glove compartment. I could just imagine the messages filling my inbox during the drive, but I managed to make it to the hotel without cracking. After dinner, she let me check my messages for ten minutes. Like a kid trying to extend their bedtime, I tried my hardest to get her to give me more time when the ten minutes were up, but she was adamant.

The next day I left my phone in the glove compartment while we enjoyed the park. I was glad to be living in the moment with my children, fully immersed in a shared experience. I noticed things about their smiles and their squeals of delight as we raced from ride to ride that I would almost certainly have missed if I'd kept my phone on me. Once again, I was given ten minutes to check my messages after dinner, but no more than this.

Late that evening, like a thief in the night, I snuck out of the condo we were renting. I sat in the car checking my emails, my heart racing at the thought of being caught. It was like being a sneaky kid again. As I walked back up to my room, though, I realized how sad this was. My mother hadn't confiscated my phone to punish me. She wanted to show me that there was a life outside of my work that demanded my attention (a life that included her, but also my children). I was missing their childhood. This was my chance to be something other than the overworked executive, and I was blowing it.

The next day I left the phone in the glovebox all day, and that night, rather than sneaking down after my mother went to bed, I stayed in my room. When everybody else had fallen asleep, I spent a moment reflecting on the kind of mother, wife, and leader I had become. I had erected barriers between my heart and my head. I was (as my team had noticed) as cold as ice, and I wasn't serving anyone (not even myself).

For a while before the Disney trip, I'd been attending national conferences. This too had given me a chance to peek out from behind the curtain. Because I was trying to be receptive to new ideas, I was open to the possibility that there might be a better way. I had convinced myself that I was the queen of the castle. I thought of myself as someone who was important, but with each conference, seminar and workshop I traveled to, my eyes were opened to entirely different ways of leading (and living) that I'd never considered. This, combined with the Disney trip, pushed me closer and closer to the larger realization that would soon wash over me.

I was still holding on to my old ways of doing and thinking with all my might, though. I remained convinced that I was where I needed to be and where others needed me to be. When I drove back to the office after my trip to Disney World, I was sure that I'd return to utter chaos. I was so important that, surely, the office would fall apart without me. It is difficult to even write these words; I see now how arrogant this was.

When I got back to the office, I quickly saw how wrong I had been. My people had gotten along just fine without me. I had half expected them to meet me at the elevator with a laundry list of issues. To my surprise, all they wanted to talk about was my trip. They asked me what I had seen and how it felt to be back.

There weren't any fires to put out—far from it. It had actually been healthy for my team not to have me at their beck and call. Although they were anxious in the beginning (a product of years of micromanagement), they quickly got used to working independently, to problem-solving on their own, to stumbling and to getting back up. They found a new sense of confidence and pride in their own abilities, and it elevated their desire to grow and contribute to the team in other ways. My need for control had created a climate in which every decision had to be double-checked. With no one to look over their shoulders, my team showed me that this had all been unnecessary.

It was just more confirmation that something needed to change. I felt different, felt refreshed and energized, and this allowed me that crucial moment of reflection. The more I thought about it, the clearer it became that I didn't have all the answers, and *I didn't have to have them.* I needed to change how I was at work and how I was at home, and I needed to become much better at properly prioritizing the two. The more I reflected, the more determined I became not to fall back into my old ways of thinking and doing.

It was my first taste of awareness. I had kept this realization at arm's length for nearly a decade, but I couldn't hold it back any longer. When I finally took a moment to reflect on the kind of leader, wife, and mother I had become, the realization that I was substantially less than I could be in all these areas fell on me like a ton of bricks.

Bringing our awareness to something and attempting to understand it are crucial, but we can't say that anything has truly *happened* until we have acted in some measurable way. Intention needs to become action—potential energy needs to become kinetic energy. I *knew* something, but things wouldn't change until I *did* something, until I actualized my potential.

Parallel Formation

The recognition that things could be better pushed me to start making changes. The more I worked on myself, the more I could see that this work was long overdue. I had convinced myself that I had all the answers, and this arrogance had informed my haughty leadership.

I had stopped growing, and growth is essential. We should never see ourselves as fully finished. The minute we stop growing, we start decaying. The instant we stop helping our teams grow, they too start to stagnate and decay. Professionally and personally, we should never stop trying to be and do better, and we should never stop trying to bring more out of our teams as well. We do this by coaching, not by commanding.

This expectation (growth both for ourselves and for those we lead) is a key component of servant leadership. Servant leaders strive for parallel formation—where leaders grow while helping those around them grow as well.

A lot of people reach their peak early. They settle into a role and stop striving for better and higher. This is as true in the C-suite as it is in the bullpen. We reach a level when, rather than striving and reaching, we plant our feet and stake our claim. This limits our personal growth, but it also limits what those around us can do.

John Maxwell calls this the Law of the Lid. In *The 21 Irrefutable Laws of Leadership* he says that leadership abilities represent a hard success ceiling, not only for you but also for the people you lead. If, for example, your leadership abilities are a seven out of ten, your success will only ever be at that middling level. What's more, you'll only ever be able to attract and lead those who are either at or below your level. The eights, nines, and tens will quickly become frustrated and move on to greener pastures.

The eights, nines, and your rock star tens are those who seek steady improvement, and they want to see the same thing in those they follow. They follow leaders who are actively engaged in parallel formation—in the ongoing attempt to improve their teams and themselves. As my daughter says, "If you want to attract a ten, you need to be a ten." If you want to surround yourself with people on an upward trajectory, they need to see the same kind of growth pattern from you.

Our teams feed off our energy and follow the example we set. The mood in the room will depend largely on the emotional state that you, the leader, bring into it. If you are having a bad day, it is highly likely that your team will have a bad day as well. You have a responsibility (for the sake of morale and performance) to do all you can to ensure you are your best self.

This all comes down to standards. Nothing stinks quite like hypocrisy and double standards. If we expect one thing for our team and another for ourselves, we'll be breeding contempt. We'll also be actively encouraging our top performers to find leaders more like themselves (i.e., consistent and kinetic).

The servant leader never hoards growth. As they grow, they encourage others to follow their example. Are you the only one who is attending conferences and educational opportunities over and above the bare minimum? Are you offering your staff these same opportunities? Are you developing yourself and then passing on insights in diluted form to your team, or are you sending your team straight to the source?

If you're not creating chances for your team to learn and grow, you're hoarding opportunities for personal and professional growth. Of course, not everybody will want this kind of development, but it should be made available to those who do. Chances are, those who seize the opportunity for personal and professional growth are your future eights, nines, and tens. Just as you look for this in them, they'll be looking for it in you.

5

Bringing Down the Walls

"Tear down the walls of Jericho. Don't remodel them."

—Tony Evans

Like so many young professionals, each time I progressed in my career, instead of growing, I built higher and thicker walls around me. I thought this was what leaders did. I thought they insulated themselves from the people around them, allowing them to make the difficult leadership decisions unemotionally.

I was not allowing myself to make genuine connections with the people I led. I could not allow myself to care for them at a deeper level—to love them—because this would expose me. It would hurt too much when I had to make the difficult decisions that would negatively affect them in a big way.

With each passing year, new walls went up: walls between me and the people I was leading; walls between my personal and professional life; walls between what I saw as professional values and my own more personal ethical code. With each new wall, the person at the center of it all (me) changed. In the end, I could barely recognize myself.

The walls were no longer simply something that protected me. They had become part of who I was, and they needed to come down.

C.S. Lewis and the Invulnerable Heart

To lead with a serving and loving heart helps us bring out the latent potential in those we lead, but it comes with steep costs. It means that we need to tear down our walls and be vulnerable—a frightening prospect for many of us.

A few years ago, I came across a passage in C.S. Lewis's *The Four Loves* that captures this idea perfectly. It's stayed with me, and I return to it frequently. Here it is in its entirety:

> *"To love at all is to be vulnerable. Love anything, and your heart will certainly be wrung and possibly broken. If you want to make sure of keeping it intact, you must give your heart to no one, not even to an animal. Wrap it carefully round with hobbies and little luxuries; avoid all entanglements; lock it up safe in the casket or coffin of your selfishness. But in that casket—safe, dark, motionless, airless—it will change. It will not be broken; it will become unbreakable; impenetrable; irredeemable."*

If we are going to lead people, we need to believe that it is toward something greater. We must believe in this so strongly that we are willing to tear down the walls we have erected around ourselves and our vulnerable hearts. We must greet the world, our arms open, our hearts exposed.

The alternative is to remain hidden within the casket of our selfishness. We may be safe and unentangled there, we may be unbreakable and impenetrable, but we are also, as Lewis says, irredeemable. Within our walls, our hearts are hardening. Pain will be alien to us, but so will love and its countless pleasures—beside which, all the world's delights pale. Safe though it might be, what kind of existence would this be? By what measure would we call this kind of life a success?

The Trumpet Blast

Love and faith in what love can accomplish are, together, the trumpet blast that brings the walls crashing down.

I want to look back to the source of the metaphor I've chosen. Joshua was a visionary leader. He understood his calling and his divinely gifted mission, and he was able to communicate his vision to his people, showing them that their efforts would be rewarded provided that they remained strong in their faith and their belief that God would deliver what he had promised his people.

Joshua led his people out of the desert and into the land promised to the Israelites, but standing between him and Canaan were the walls of Jericho. Cannons and catapults didn't bring down the walls of Jericho—it was the Israelites' voices raised to the heavens combined with the sound of their trumpets that crumbled the city's impenetrable defenses.

The Israelites' faith gave the sound of their voices and their trumpets power. Your faith in what love can accomplish can do the same. When the walls come down, you may feel naked and defenseless, but you will be instilled with a new kind of strength—the strength of loving and of being loved (stronger by far than the autocrat's hammer). This is the strength that can pull down the walls we have built around ourselves but also the walls that others have built around themselves. It requires that we be vulnerable, but this is the only way we can see and be seen by those around us. We can't love what we can't see—at best we can admire from a distance. To love someone is to know them, to know them is to love them.

Becoming the kind of leader who builds off a foundation like this takes a tremendous amount of courage. Gird up your loins and brace yourself. Believe wholeheartedly in the power of love. Blow that trumpet with everything you've got and watch the walls come tumbling down.

The Walls of Monica

I used to carry two cell phones with me at all times: a work phone and a personal phone. There was no overlap between the two phones. My personal life and my work life couldn't have been more completely separated.

No one from the office saw the inside of my home. I told my colleagues next to nothing about my personal life. This kind of openness would, I thought, damage my credibility. After all, I was a simple country girl who had found success in the corporate world. Growing up, we did not meet the financial criteria to receive government assistance (not that my mom would have accepted it). At the same time, we didn't have a penny to spare. I started my professional career with a bare minimum of schooling (just a two-year college degree).

My suit and heels were a disguise. Beneath the makeup and the professional veneer was, I thought, an impostor. I was convinced that if I laid all my cards on the table, no one would take me seriously.

Away from the office, it was the same feeling but in reverse. My mother and sisters are all nurses. They called the administrative and executive staff who would walk down the halls of the hospital in their suits and heels *clackers*. I was one of those clackers, and the way they talked about administrators made me feel like a traitor—like I wasn't being true to my nursing roots. I didn't feel like they were describing me when they talked about some of the worst clackers in the hospital, but in these conversations, I often felt like I was defending myself. My mother and sisters joked with me, saying that I didn't have the stomach for nursing work. I questioned whether I lacked that other key component of the nursing profession: care and compassion for the sufferings of others.

I was born and raised in a Catholic home, and, if asked, I would have said that I was living my Christian values at home and at work, but a part of me knew that I had built walls around some of my most deeply held beliefs. As I advanced professionally, I behaved less and less like a good Christian and more and more like a numbers-driven boss, putting the needs of the organization before the human needs of its people.

One moment from early in my career stands out to me. I had made a bad hire. The employee was not the right fit for either the position or the organization. I saw no other option but termination. The chair didn't stay empty for long, though. I had a replacement waiting in the wings. I told my boss about my decision, saying that we would have to wait and see how the new hire would work out.

"Now you're talking like a manager," he said.

I was puzzled. "What do you mean?" I asked.

"You've always been too optimistic," he said. "You should always assume the worst. You're going to need to become a lot more jaded if you are going to make it in this business."

His comment struck me, and I remember rolling it over in my mind for weeks. Each time I felt like someone deserved my trust, I returned to his words. Each time someone let me down, I remembered what he said and reminded myself not to be too optimistic about my people.

The more I gave up on my optimism, the more my skepticism deepened. The walls around me grew thicker with each passing day. I gave few people the benefit of the doubt. Instead, I demanded they prove themselves over and over again before I gave them my trust (which was only ever bestowed provisionally). I was, I told myself, thinking like a manager.

When the Walls Came Down

On July 30th, 2013, my nine-year-old son and his fourteen-year-old brother took our golf cart out with some of the other neighborhood children. It was a balmy summer evening, and their carefree spirits got the best of them. My youngest was sitting on the front of the cart while they drove it back home. They hit a bump and he couldn't hold on. He fell into the cart's path and was run over.

Minutes later, my eldest burst in the door carrying his battered and bloody brother in his arms. After some emergency triage in the bathroom, we took him to the hospital. His injuries were extensive. He had a broken clavicle, two collapsed lungs, a ruptured spleen, and multiple contusions across his pelvis and legs. He looked as though he'd been scalped, and his muscle tissue was so damaged across his midsection that we were worried the cart might have crushed his pelvis. When the X-rays came back, we breathed a sigh of relief. By the grace of God, the only bone he'd broken was his clavicle.

We still didn't know, though, if there were any internal injuries. My husband and I stood together and watched the nurses and doctors tend to our boy, both of us trying to remain cautiously optimistic while we awaited the results of his scans.

With the results in hand, the doctors told us that he needed to be transported to the nearest pediatric trauma unit. It was a long two weeks of ups and downs, but the doctors frequently gave us assurances that he would make a full recovery, though it would take time. He would have a few battle wounds and some permanent scars, but, other than that, he would be no worse for wear.

Three days after the accident, I was standing in the hall outside my son's hospital room. I was still wearing the same blood-spattered clothes I had been wearing when we arrived at the hospital. It had been days since I had showered or even run a brush through my hair. Miss Corporate America was nowhere to be found.

From the corner of my eye, I spotted what seemed to be a familiar face. It was the new youth minister from our church whom I had met (only briefly) the month before. I turned towards him and we made eye contact. There was so much care and compassion in his expression, so much human sympathy in his eyes, that I was caught completely off guard. I was unprepared for the wave of emotions. I tried to keep them back, but it was no use. The walls came tumbling down. As he hugged me and prayed for my son and me, I cried uncontrollably. The river of emotion that I had been holding back for God knows how long broke its banks and covered everything.

To this day, the memory of that moment still brings tears to my eyes. I cannot remember what he said, but it wasn't what was said: it was the feeling behind it. I ugly cried all over the front of his shirt—tears, snot, the works. He waited patiently until I was composed enough to form a coherent sentence. We talked, and he helped me find a place of calm in the midst of fear and uncertainty. Standing before me was a spiritual companion who would, in both word and deed, stand by me in my hour of need. I didn't need to walk alone. He offered to walk beside me.

Later, when I reflected on this moment, I remembered his compassion and how it made me feel in my moment of need. This was an example of the kind of servant leadership I was striving for. There was a softness to his approach that encouraged vulnerability. I was not expected to *get over it* or to *be strong*. Instead, I was encouraged to submit to my feelings and, by submitting to them, to pass through them.

He showed me the way forward, but he didn't push or pull me down the path. I had to walk it myself. He served me by helping me to serve myself.

6

Leading with Love

"Leadership without love is manipulation."

—Rick Warren

When we lead from a place of love, when we show our people care and patience and a genuine interest in their wellbeing, they will, in their own time, return that love. We can't expect or demand their love (this is what dictators do). We need to show them that we deserve their love. It starts with us, with that loving spark.

We set the spark to the kindling by being the kind of leader who is worthy of their love. This starts with demonstrating to our people that we're leading them with the right purpose. Why do you want to lead? Is it for power or prestige? If so, you'll only ever have as much support from your people as you demand—and often not even that much. If you insist on putting profit before people, you'll never be a servant leader. If your people's hopes and aspirations are only important when they align neatly with your goals and the organization's bottom line, you aren't a servant leader. You aren't leading people, you're using them.

If, however, you want to lead because you want to help your organization *and* its people grow, you have the potential to become a servant leader.

If you want to taste authentic influence (the kind that servant leaders enjoy), you need more than power. You need to be surrounded by people who respect and trust you, and that starts with them knowing who you are. They need to know the *real* you, not some version of yourself that you have constructed to fill a role.

Think of the people in your life who you would follow to the ends of the earth. Are these people unknowable, aloof, or inaccessible? Chances are, they are exactly the opposite. You trust them and follow them because you feel you know them. They are open books, open doors, open hearts. You know their motivations are pure, and you know they would not step over you to further their own interests.

Ask yourself: Can your people say the same thing about you? Do they know you or only some version of you-as-leader that you've constructed for them? Do they trust you (enough to follow you to the ends of the earth)? Do they know you have their best interests at heart? Are you an open book, an open door, an open heart? Do you love them, and do they love you in return?

Choosing Love

Contrary to what many may think, love is not just a feeling, it is also an action. It is a choice that we make each and every day, and one we make actively not passively (i.e., we make it ourselves—it isn't made for us).

Love is constant. It's a choice we make day after day, and choosing love is easier some days than others. This is how we encounter and overcome obstacles together—by making that actionable decision day in and day out. We adopt the servant's position by choosing love, even when making that decision is harder than surrendering to our darker impulses.

When we make this decision—and keep making it—our care radiates out of us. It's impossible to miss. This is what St. Thomas Aquinas was talking about when he said, "To love is to will the good for the other." Aquinas wasn't talking about romantic love but, rather, about authentic love. This kind of love asks for nothing in return. It simply *is*. It exists outside of the laws of reciprocity. It is pure benevolence.

The true servant leader asks, "What can I give?" not "What can I get?" When we ask this question, we have chosen love, have chosen to serve rather than command.

This is easier—much, much easier—when we are dealing with an employee who is a perfect fit both with us and with the organization. The challenge comes when you are tasked with leading someone who fits uneasily with you or the organization. When they make a mistake, or when there's a difference of opinion strong enough to produce a conflict, it is easier to fall back into patterns of mistrust and fruitless criticism.

Often, when there is a behavioral problem with an employee, the issue is rooted in something beneath the surface. There's something going on with them, either at home, at the office, or somewhere between. They might be struggling with their spouse, a child, a friend, or a relation, or there might be an issue with interpersonal dynamics in the workplace. You can only address what happens in the workplace, but no matter where the root of their issue is, you can and should provide your people with the space and the comfort they need to unburden themselves. More often than not, they will reveal to you what the problem is if you're patient enough to *really listen.*

Ask yourself how you can help them. What is truly best for them in that moment? In some cases, what is best for them might be moving on, but this should not be a first resort. Termination is only appropriate when it's absolutely clear that their needs and the organization's and its people's needs are incompatible.

The servant leader does all they can to prevent things from reaching this boiling point. The solution is often (like love itself) quite simple. It might be some time off to address personal issues, mediation between them and other staff, or it might be a transfer that eases some of the interpersonal friction. Whatever the solution, it never involves turning your back on them (especially not when they are in their hour of need).

Reciprocal Love

We cannot truly and deeply love those we do not know truly and deeply. While we seek to know and understand members of our team so that we might lovingly lead them, we should be looking for opportunities to make this understanding reciprocal. If we are to lead lovingly, we need to know our people, but it is equally important that they know us.

If we choose to keep our walls up, never giving our people a glimpse behind the curtain, they will be unable to love us in return. All healthy and mutually beneficial relationships are reciprocal. Without allowing their love to flow back toward us, we are in essence rejecting them. We are closing off the possibility that they can feel that deep sense of belonging—as though they are part of our tribe.

When I was still a young professional, I attended a women's leadership conference. A woman stepped to the podium and began speaking about how we should be conducting ourselves within our organizations. "Never let them see you cry!" she said. "I don't care what you have to do. Go into the bathroom, lock yourself up in your car for a while, but NEVER let them see you cry!" I took this message to heart, carrying it with me for years. I wanted to check off all the boxes, to do all the things that good leaders do, so I followed her advice. I closed myself off, building higher and higher walls around my heart.

The connections between us are essential to leadership. These connections *must* go in both directions. We must seek to better understand our people and connect with them in ways that move beyond the superficial, but we must also allow them to broach our defenses and reach that inner sanctum. Present yourself as the unflexing image of stoicism and your people will never connect with you on an emotional level. They are more likely to see you as an object or a symbol than as a caring and loving person. It took me years to learn this lesson.

In 2010, I joined an organization in a leadership role. The problems the organization was facing were so large, the environment so toxic, that nothing less than an aggressive intervention would get things moving in the right direction. I plowed ahead, implementing the changes I thought were essential without taking the time to listen to the opinions of those around me.

I was convinced that, with an act of will, I could straighten the bent rod. There would be no more gossip, no more infighting. I was in charge now, and things were going to change. The choice was simple: either get on board or jump ship. More people than I expected headed for the exits, but I brushed this off as necessary, telling myself that we were losing dead weight.

There was good with the bad. I did some of the difficult but necessary interpersonal work to smooth some of the bumps in the culture out, and I encouraged healthier team dynamics and better practices by introducing gamification, which got people smiling and laughing together, enhancing morale overnight and creating bonds where there had once been conflicts.

I was still doing most of this from behind the curtain. I tried to get the team to drop their guard and let me in, but I didn't reciprocate. My energies only ever flowed in one direction.

I attempted to connect with them, but I didn't allow them to connect with me. I shared some laughs with some of them and, at times, I treated members of the team to appetizers and cocktails after work as a reward for reaching a milestone or hitting a specified target. However, I did not want them to see me as anything other than their confident leader. I rarely talked about my personal life beyond surface level stuff, and I never let my emotions show. I went through the motions of friendly office relations, but that's all. They never got a glimpse of the real me behind the curtain.

One morning, the phone rang in my office. It was Shanna, one of our nurses, who typically would be out making home visits at that time. She was crying uncontrollably. Between sobs, she managed to tell me the reason for her call: "I need some employment documentation to bring with me to the hospital," she said. I was confused. At first, I thought she was talking about one of her patients she was seeing that day, but it turned out she wasn't with a patient. She was driving herself to the hospital.

Shanna had been on the way to see a patient when her phone had started ringing. It was her doctor, and he told her to get herself to the hospital immediately. Some routine scans had turned up what looked like a brain tumor, and it was imperative that she get herself to the hospital for further testing. Shanna said she was going to swing by the office and grab the necessary documentation on her way to the hospital. I told her that I would gather the documents myself and bring them downstairs.

A few minutes later, I was in the parking lot with the documents in hand. When she arrived, I could see immediately that she was still distraught. Her eyes were filled with tears, and she was struggling to get her words out. She was in no shape to drive, and I told her so. I ushered her into my car and drove her to the hospital.

I spent the day at Shanna's side. There were more tests to run, more doctors to see, and a whole lot of waiting to do. Through it all, I tried to keep her calm and assure her that she was in good hands. For the most part, though, we simply sat together in silence. I gave her my hand to hold, and she took it. We sat there, hand in hand, watching a closed door and waiting for it to open. With her hand in mine, I prayed silently for good news.

After what felt like a lifetime, the door finally opened, and someone called her name. They brought her to an exam room and told us the doctor would be with us shortly. After what seemed like another eternity in that small room, a doctor came in looking over her test results. There had, she said, been a mistake. It was not a brain tumor. There were other issues, but none of them life-threatening. The doctor discussed the next steps with Shanna and told her she could go home.

I drove her back to her car and, with her assurances that she was okay to drive, I told her to go straight home and get some rest. "Work can wait," I said. "I'll call you tomorrow to check on how you're doing." She thanked me and, with a wave, drove off.

I went back up to the office, where two of the staff members were waiting for my return. They wanted to know what had happened, and they were clearly concerned about Shanna. I stood in the doorway of the office for a moment. I had planned to give them a no-nonsense update on her status, but as soon as I opened my mouth, my hands began to shake and my voice broke. The curtain went up. For the first time, they got a glimpse of the real me.

I choked on my words, and tears welled up in my eyes. Something passed between us, something entirely new. They both immediately shot up from their desks and crossed the room towards me, and I could see deep concern written on their faces—concern for Shanna, but also for me. With some effort, I managed to get the words out. "She's going to be fine," I said, "it was a misdiagnosis."

A wave of relief went through the room. My tears had, they said, confused them. They'd never seen me show emotion like this, so they assumed it meant that something was terribly wrong with Shanna. They were happy to hear that she was okay, but they weren't smiling yet. They wanted to know if I was okay.

"I know y'all think I'm made of ice, but I really do care about all of you," I said.

They gathered around me and gave me hugs, trying to comfort me. My tears dried, and I began to compose myself. Sniffing, I told them with a little grin that I'd fire anyone who let it be known that I broke down in tears.

Needless to say, the news spread. The next day, a number of people came in to ask about Shanna, and, when I told them that it had been a false alarm, many of them lingered. Some of them asked me about how the day had affected me, others just made small talk. It was the beginning of something. I had shown vulnerability, and my team members responded by opening the door to deeper levels of connection.

I'm still friends with several people from that organization. For most of them, that day is the one we both point to as the true relationship starting point. Our team grew more unified that day. They began to trust me more, especially when we faced difficult situations. I was more open with them, and they with me.

When I had first taken the reins, I had been too willful, too firm, too controlled. Now, they could see that, behind the curtain, I was more sensitive than I had let on. They saw that I felt for them, and in that moment (perhaps for the first time) they felt for me. I let my guard down, and they reciprocated.

We moved forward from that day with a new understanding of each other. Finally, we were moving forward *together.*

Conduit for Connection

Loving those you lead means opening yourself up to connecting on a human-to-human level. Communication is the conduit for these connections, but we need to communicate mindfully. We must speak in a language that is understood, and we must also listen carefully and, through careful listening, try to understand.

Communication breakdowns are often a result of an inability or an unwillingness to understand each other—to really listen to what the other person is saying. We expect to be heard, but we won't hear others. We expect others to adapt to our preferred style of communication rather than being, ourselves, adaptable.

We've all been in conversations with poor communicators, and we've all (if we're honest) been bad communicators at some point. Rather than using communication as a conduit for connection, we simply wait for our turn to talk (or yell). This kind of inflexibility and willful deafness is one of the hallmarks of autocratic leaders. Servant leaders listen and take on board what they are hearing (both text and subtext).

This is not something we're born with. It's something we mature into. It's not natural. It demands intention and effort. It can evoke emotions we may not be comfortable with as we step into areas of vulnerability. Really listening often means admitting that we don't have all the answers and recognizing our blind spots.

If you find yourself repeating the same things over and over, if you find that the people around you just don't *get it*, you may have a communication problem. You may need to learn to communicate in a different way, beginning with listening. If you have a problem with everyone, the problem may not be everyone, it may be you. You're the common denominator.

Communication Breakdowns

When leaders don't get the results they want, it is often a result of their failure to communicate effectively. One of the main issues I encounter over and over again is a defensiveness surrounding their own miscommunications. This means responses like, "That is not what I meant!" or "You don't get it!"—both symptoms of poor top-down communication.

Each conversation is an opportunity to get on or stay on the same page. If you stray from that page, the fault might be theirs, or it might be yours. Most likely, though, is that you share the fault. You're on different pages because there's been a communication breakdown on both sides.

The other person is filtering what you say through lenses ground and shaped by their experiences and emotions, and you are doing the same. Effective communication breaks free from this and hears what is *actually* said—not what we expect or want to hear. Effective communicators are patient, waiting to move on until it is clear that what they're saying or what they're hearing is being received precisely as intended.

When communicating, try to spend more time listening than speaking. Pay careful attention and read between the lines. Hear what is being said, but also what is being left unsaid. Repeat what the other person has said back to them in their own words, and then translate that into your own words. Don't move on until it's crystal clear that there is a mutual understanding.

By demonstrating listening skills, you'll be teaching them as well. Be curious in conversations with your people. Do this actively and passionately and they'll respond with curiosity of their own. When we actively show them that we are listening, they tend to return the favor and pay it forward.

How do we actively show curiosity? With our faces. We can all tell when we are talking to someone who isn't really listening. They've checked out of the conversation. We might as well be talking to a brick wall. Few things are more frustrating than this for those who feel the point they are making is important.

We can show we're engaged by leaning forward, by showing interest with our facial expressions. Of course, we should close our mouths and listen, but this doesn't mean becoming a passive participant in the conversation. Even something as simple as nodding at key points in the conversation will make it clear that you're hearing and taking in what they're saying.

I've found that when I make my listening and engagement active like this, the conversation begins to crackle with life. Ideas flow rapidly back and forth, and the conversations are far more productive. Conversations with active curiosity at their center produce results.

This is not something that comes easy. It requires practice, but this practice is an opportunity to learn more about your communication preferences and those of others.

Loving and Leading Languages

The languages of servant leadership and love mirror each other. Both languages speak of putting other people's needs ahead of our own. Both speak about aligned goals and visions. Both attempt to find a path forward that allows for personal *and* mutual growth.

Love and servant leadership both seek a way to locate and then develop the best versions of ourselves. Both do this with compassion, kindness, and careful listening. The success of the unit (either the couple or the organization) is measured by its ability to allow *all* those within its circle to flourish. Failures and successes are always shared.

What does this language sound like? What kind of things do servant leaders say? To find an answer, we can look to what St. Paul says about love in his letters to the Corinthians.

Before Paul's conversion on the road to Damascus, he had been an influential Jewish leader. As a Pharisee, he and his party were the most well-respected interpreters of the Jewish laws, and he applied their interpretation with a heavy hand. When his early attempts to force Christians to abandon their "heretical" beliefs failed, he had many of them tortured and killed.

After his conversion, though, Paul adopted an approach more in line with the teachings of the one who appeared before him in a vision on the road to Damascus. Following Christ's example, he shaped and corrected his followers and the young church through love and influence. He didn't tyrannize. He led.

Love was the cornerstone of his faith, and, in 1 Corinthians 13:1, he admonished those who would speak even His words without love: "If I speak in human and angelic tongues, but do not have love, I am a resounding gong or a clanging cymbal." Without love, our language is hollow. It rings out, but it contains no substance. It does not linger in the mind of its hearers or touch their hearts. Like the sound of a gong or a cymbal, it is noise without purpose.

Paul followed this with a lengthy definition of what love is and is not. We have grown used to hearing this list read aloud at weddings, but I've always found his words particularly illuminating when they are applied in a leadership context. When you're thinking about how to apply the principles of loving servant leadership, think of Paul's words:

"Love is patient"

Servant leaders learn how to master "practicing the pause". Rather than reacting impulsively, they pause and consider how to respond appropriately. Servant leaders also allow those they lead to grow at their own pace. They remain patient while others grow, and, when necessary, they gently support and encourage those who've fallen behind, helping them catch up to the group.

"Love is kind"

Servant leaders do not shy away from difficult decisions and conversations, but they make sure to approach these conversations with kindness in their hearts. They want to see their organizations improve, but they don't let this overrun their desire to help bring the best out of those they lead.

"Love is not jealous"

Servant leaders do not envy or resent those they lead. They freely provide opportunities, even when they know that those they lead may, in time, outgrow them. In fact, they actually seek out people to bring onto their team who have the potential to do so, graciously celebrating their growth and advancement.

"Love is not pompous"

Servant leaders do not seek to stoke their own fires but to fan the fires of those they lead. They graciously lift and affirm those they lead rather than seeking recognition for themselves. They put *we* before *me*.

"Love is not inflated"

Servant leaders bring hope while remaining grounded in reality. They do not exaggerate accomplishments to make themselves look more important or more accomplished than they are. They present themselves (and see themselves) in their true colors.

"Love is not rude"

Servant leaders treat everyone around them with dignity and respect regardless of their station. They would rather honor the lowly than inflate the proud few. They are honest and direct, but never rude or cruel.

"Love does not seek its own interest"

Servant leaders consider the situational impact of all people involved and affected—not just their own. They know that their own success is predicated on the success of those they lead.

"Love is not quick tempered"

Servant leaders are the calm in the storm—never the storm itself. They are disciplined with their emotions and do not lash out from fear, frustration or anger. They respond calmly and respectfully, even in the midst of chaos.

"Love does not brood over injury"

Servant leaders are quick to move on. They do not dwell on setbacks or get swept away by personal conflicts. If they are wounded, they allow the wound (and the relationship) time to heal.

“Love does not rejoice over wrongdoing but rejoices with the truth”

Servant leaders have a strong moral compass. They encourage those they lead to walk the straight and narrow path of righteousness, and they celebrate uprightness. When evaluating an action, they look deeper than legality, deeper than permission. They want to know if it is the right thing to do.

Love “bears all things”

Servant leaders bear responsibility for their own actions and decisions, but also for those of the team they lead. When something goes wrong, they are the first to accept the blame. When things go right, they are just as quick to share the recognition.

Love “believes all things”

Servant leaders give the benefit of the doubt to those they lead. They are not gullible, but they will sooner trust than suspect. They have faith.

Love “hopes all things”

Servant leaders are confident that the future can be and will be better. Their hope is infectious. Those they lead share their vision of a better future.

Love “endures all things”

Servant leaders provide a lasting image of true leadership. They are there for those they lead through thick and thin. Whenever possible, they make of their backs a porch under which their teams can take cover.

Are you leading with love? I encourage you to go back through this list that St. Paul gives us and insert your name in place of the word love. If you can say all of the above about yourself, you are leading with love. You are a servant leader.

Love is More than Words

I want to close this chapter with a brief reminder that loving language needs to have its counterpart in loving actions. When what we say and what we do are misaligned, our words become St. Paul's gong or cymbal. They are empty, meaningless, white noise. Even when we mean what we say, we'll be greeted with suspicion. We'll have to prove our goodwill over and over again.

Remember, love is not just a noun. It is also a verb. It's not just something you give or receive, and it's definitely not just something you say, it's something you *do*.

We need to do this with all our heart, embracing those we lead in their totality. Just as we love our mates holistically (finding even their flaws lovable), we need to lead the entire person. We must recognize that those we lead are comprised of mind, body, and spirit. Servant leaders keep this insight close to their heart. They try to look through surfaces to see the complex and multi-faceted individual beneath the skin. Those they lead feel completely *seen,* and they respond by giving themselves completely.

Words	Action
"Good job!"	During a team meeting, acknowledge their accomplishment and its importance.
"I believe in you."	Provide them with an opportunity to grow their skills without micromanaging them.
"I'm here to support you."	Help them prepare for an important presentation, then be present for the presentation. Lend them moral support without drawing attention to yourself.
"You are important. Your perspective is valuable."	Sit beside them in a meeting rather than assuming the power position behind your desk. Treat them as an equally valuable human.
"I understand."	Implement changes based on their insights or suggestions.

7

Emotional Intelligence from Scratch

"People don't care how much you know
until they know how much you care."

–John C. Maxwell

Successful leaders possess broad skill sets. They are expected to be able to strategize, communicate, and navigate, but, more than this, they are expected to have those more-difficult-to-define *people skills*. All too often, new leaders arrive in their position with under-developed skills of this kind. They come to understand the importance of people skills either too late or never.

They may try to connect emotionally with their team, but something stands in their way. The barrier is almost always a single deficit: Leaders may have a high IQ, but too often they lack emotional intelligence (EQ). Our IQ allows us to lead from our head. Our EQ allows us to lead from our heart. It takes both head and heart to lead effectively.

Emotional intelligence means an ability to fully understand our own emotions and the role they play in our actions, but also the corresponding ability to understand the emotions of others. It means understanding that what we see is only a portion of the iceberg. The vast majority of our motivations lie below the waterline, and emotionally intelligent people know they need to look beneath to understand both what has happened and the emotional state (*the why*) behind it.

In this chapter, we'll be looking at the two kinds of awareness that, together, create emotional intelligence: self-awareness and social awareness.

Self-Awareness: Gazing Inward

As with most things, becoming a better leader starts with a look inward. We need to work on and with ourselves, but this is easier said than done. We might just be the hardest person we ever have to work with.

We need to bring an intentionality to this process. Working on ourselves takes time and effort. It's not a program that can be running in the background. We need to actively direct and participate in this process.

This starts with something relatively simple, with naming the emotions we are experiencing (good and bad). We ask ourselves the following question:

What am I feeling right now?

Having the ability to recognize and assign a name to the emotions we are experiencing in any given situation provides us with the capacity to control and express our emotions judiciously and empathetically.

We have to understand what is inside of us to recognize what is coming out of us. If we are unable to identify what we are feeling and why, we won't be able to understand (at least not fully) how we are impacting others. We'll be more likely to miss the glaringly obvious fact that what we project often comes bouncing back at us. If we project anger and distrust, we can't expect patience or faith in return.

This will also train us how to better understand others. When we start understanding how our emotions translate into our behaviors, we can start to gain a deeper understanding of what drives others to behave as they do. With this understanding, we are far more likely to treat others with empathy. We have a common emotional reference point.

Our Triggers

We all have triggers. We tend to think of these in purely negative terms. When we say we feel *triggered*, we generally mean that someone has pushed our buttons and produced a negative emotional response.

I want to open this idea up. Yes, we can be negatively triggered, but we can use the term to describe something positive as well. I may, for instance, be negatively triggered when a peer brags about receiving a promotion that I wanted myself. It may trigger anger and jealousy, and, if I allow myself to be carried away by these emotions, I may end up saying or doing something I will regret later. It's an important part of EQ to be able to recognize when we've been negatively triggered in this way.

In the same way, I might be positively triggered when I am recognized in front of my peers. I might feel seen and valued if this recognition comes from a superior, and this goes double when we feel that their praise is sincere.

It's important to remember how it feels to be positively and negatively triggered. Servant leaders strive to positively trigger those they lead. Praise is one of the biggest positive triggers, so rather than withholding praise, a true servant leader seeks out opportunities to affirm and recognize others' contributions.

When we pull these positive triggers, those we lead feel seen and acknowledged, valued and appreciated. The more often we do this, the more leeway we'll be given when it comes time to pull those negative triggers (news cannot always be good). If every time they open your door, you push their buttons, they'll develop a hair trigger. A single word or a look can be enough to put them in that defensive position. If we pull their positive triggers regularly, they'll be more receptive when we have to deliver bad news or a critique.

Developing emotional intelligence is all about awareness and discipline. Exercising this intelligence gives us the ability to choose (as much as possible) how we respond to a given situation, but it's also about managing how others respond. We're not *telling* them how to respond; we're influencing their response and guiding each engagement towards a positive outcome.

Some emotions can be almost impossible to control, so it won't always work. You may overreact when your buttons are pushed a little (or a lot) too hard, or you may provoke a strongly negative reaction. In both cases, though, you can, through awareness and understanding, salvage what is salvageable. With a patient and loving approach, cooler heads will soon prevail.

I want to pause here for a moment because this point is crucial. There is *nothing* wrong with strong emotional responses. Emotional intelligence is about awareness, not about bottling your passion. When harnessed, passion makes people more eager to follow our lead—especially when they see that at the heart of your passion is a desire to serve others.

Self-Awareness: The Autobiographical Business Plan

We can use the same techniques that we use to understand our businesses that we use to understand ourselves. Let's say that you wanted to create a successful business. The first concrete step would be to craft a business plan. In the same way, we can create an autobiographical business plan that will help us better understand ourselves and our emotions.

A good business plan starts with research. We need data, and the more of it the better. We need to understand how the market has moved and will move, and we need to understand how our product or service will fit into these movements. We need to understand our competitors, both in terms of what they have that we don't and vice versa. We need to do a S.W.O.T. analysis, looking at the strengths, weaknesses, opportunities, and threats that lie ahead for our business.

In the same way, we need to research ourselves, and this means much more than knowing our biographical details. We need to know what makes us tick at a deeper level. As I said above, this starts with naming the emotions we're feeling when we're feeling them. This allows us to start mapping our emotional selves.

Don't limit your research to your emotional self, though. Be sure to also consider your body and how it reacts. When you are under pressure, do you get hot? Does this feeling of heat provoke a certain emotional response? Are you, for instance, quick to lose your patience when you can feel the tips of your ears burning?

All of this is part of the map of ourselves that we're trying to draw. The more detailed our map is, the more it will yield to the kind of in-depth analysis we need to do. We need to analyze the data and try to predict potential outcomes (this kind of predictive power is, after all, what we hope a business plan will give us).

Now you can start analyzing the data and making some predictions. If A occurs and I do X, will the result be positive or negative? How will the outcome change if, instead of doing X, I do Y? If Y produces the best outcomes, how can I make sure that, when A occurs, I always do Y?

Just as with a business plan, when you chart your course through possibilities and alternatives like this, you are better prepared for the future and what it might bring. External factors no longer feel like they are out of your control when you have considered the possibilities and have planned a response ahead of time.

Businesses that don't start with a concrete and carefully researched business plan are far more likely to go down in flames. When we ignore our emotions and our emotional triggers, we are exposing ourselves to similar risks. When the pressures rise, our emotions might carry us to places we don't want to go. By ignoring or suppressing our emotions, we've placed ourselves entirely in their power. When we do this, we are not eliminating emotional pain—only deferring it. Sooner or later, we'll have to pay the piper.

Fixing our emotional issues means experiencing the emotions we might rather leave buried. You can't begin to address these issues from the outside. You have to get in there and roll around in it. Those high walls you've built around you are on the outside. They keep other people out, but you're trapped behind them. You're looking outwards, through holes in the wall. You're only getting a partial picture of what's going on outside, but you're not really turning around and looking around inside either. Emotional intelligence work means turning your back to the wall and starting to explore the space inside your own head.

When you start doing this work, the people around you will notice. Leading by example goes a long way, and there's no better way to lead by example than to lead yourself. Don't keep your self-awareness work to yourself. Tell people what you're doing. Talk about how it's changing you. The more the people around you start to see the benefits of this kind of work, the more likely it becomes that they will at least consider doing some similar work themselves. As this spreads from person to person, the organization's strength is multiplied ten-fold. A team full of people who've honed their emotional intelligence can accomplish remarkable things together.

Social Awareness: Gazing Outward

While we are working on developing our self-awareness, we can also start expanding our social awareness. This means starting to understand that we are *all* emotionally driven creatures.

It only takes a moment to see the truth of this. Look around a room that is filled with people. For just a few seconds, look closely at some of them. Each of them is communicating silently with body language. A foot bouncing under the table, hands fiddling with the hem of a skirt—these are outward displays of inward emotional states. We can start to become more socially aware by paying attention to these little things, by looking for the little details. If we look and listen carefully, we'll start to see through the action to the emotional reality behind it. We'll *see* how they're feeling.

When we start watching and listening more carefully, we start to fire up our empathy engines. It's only then that we can start to act on our understanding of what others are feeling. It's only then we can start *showing* that we care about others and are concerned about their welfare.

Like anything, social awareness and the empathy it produces are skills that we can develop. Some of us are born empathetic, but, for most of us, empathy is something we develop—sometimes with great effort. Empathic people tend to view situations from the perspective of how the issue is affecting all parties involved.

If you want to get better at this, the next time you have to make a decision that involves someone else, take some time (more than a few moments) to really consider their perspective. How would you feel if you were in their shoes? If you think they will be pleased with the outcome, how do you know this for sure? Might you be making assumptions about what they want? Is there a way to balance your needs with theirs?

Getting into the habit of asking questions like these is a great way to build empathy. You might not be able to answer all the questions you ask, but even non-answers are instructive. These are your blind spots, the gaps in your understanding that you can attempt to fill the next time you meet with the person in question.

How to Build Empathy

- Seek out and embrace failure: Get outside of your comfort zone. Try something that needs time and effort to master. Experience with failure makes us more compassionate towards those who are struggling or failing.
- Broaden your horizons: Travel to new places and meet new people. Nothing sharpens communication skills like trying to be understood when there is no common language.
- Get curious: Ask questions. Lots of them. Try to move beyond the what to the why.

Remember, empathy isn't about having all the answers; it's about caring enough to ask the question.

Communication Skills: Moving from the Vicious to the Virtuous

While a vast assortment of skills falls under the large umbrella of what we call leadership, the servant leader is particularly adept at what we might call human connection skills—the skills that underpin healthy human relationships. Servant leaders are either born with or learn to sharpen these skills because they know that these skills are the path to the best versions of ourselves. They also know that these skills help us bring out the best in others.

These human connection skills are transferable in ways that other leadership skills are not. Knowing how to balance a spreadsheet or how to delegate responsibilities might be indispensable in the boardroom but, in the tighter circles of loved ones and friends, they have limited applications. However, when it is relational capital that we are building, human connection skills are universal currency: they're valued at all times and in all places.

Like emotional intelligence, human connection skills aren't immediately obvious. They come to the surface when we display strength of character and virtue. If you are unsure whether you have these or not, ask yourself whether your behaviors are magnetic or repulsive. Do they draw people closer, or do they create distance? Are you an open door or a closed one? Are you an oasis in the desert or a red-hot poker?

Toxic leaders and the toxic cultures they preside over are anchored in the vices. They are vicious of spirit—prideful, envious, and wrathful—and they are vicious in body—slothful, greedy, gluttonous, and lustful. These vices are all repulsive. They create emotional distance and reinforce social inequalities that have no place in office politics.

Vicious cultures reward bad actors (especially those in positions of authority), which makes them extremely difficult to uproot. Some would rather leave the status quo alone. Those who cling to the status quo might not admit it, but they prefer toxic workplaces. They benefit from them either spiritually or materially. The status quo might feel as though it has roots that extend all the way to the center of the earth, but, as history shows us, the status quo *will* move—but not without collective effort.

Servant leaders are up for this challenge. They set the example by anchoring their conduct in virtues, and they do the same with the cultures they preside over. This often means a dramatic culture change. Replacing a vicious culture with a virtuous one is a tall order, but, over and over again, I've seen what can happen when the leader is determined to permanently solve their leadership and culture problems. Providing an example is a good start, but it's not enough. The servant leader can be a model of humility, kindness, patience, diligence, charity, temperance, and chastity, but being virtuous is not enough on its own. We must also do everything within our power to help those we lead develop and exhibit these virtues.

This is where our communication skills come into play. No matter how forcefully you address your people, you cannot command them to be better. You need to *influence* them to be better. I've found that focusing on three key areas can dramatically improve communication and your ability to move people with your words:

1) Bring each encounter your *complete* focus: Ineffective communicators are never fully present. You can tell that they are thinking about something else. Their eyes dart about the room, or they glance down at the phone frequently. Treat every moment to communicate as an opportunity to deepen a relationship.
2) Ask open-ended questions: If every question you ask has a yes/no answer, you're not really encouraging them to enter the conversation in any significant way. String closed-ended questions together and you'll quickly feel their focus moving elsewhere. You need to be present, but this isn't enough. You also need to do everything you can to keep them present in the moment and attuned to what you're communicating.
3) Get on the same page: This doesn't have to mean that you have complete agreement—only that you understand each other. If you're communicating expectations or critiquing, take time at key points in the conversation to make sure that what you're communicating is clear. Rather than asking them if they understand, ask them to sum things up in their own words.

The best communicators use influence, not orders. Listen carefully and speak respectfully. Speak to your people in a language they can understand. When you connect with them and your message resonates, barriers will disappear. You'll be able to move forward as one body.

Servant Leaders: Multi-focal

Servant leaders are able to balance different perspectives. They are multi-focal, able to see that perspectives (including their own) change everything. They are self-aware—or at least self-aware enough to know when they're being led by their emotions. They are also socially aware—or at least socially aware enough to recognize that their perspective is not universal.

Servant leaders know that the key to effective leadership is the ability to find a balance between their own perspective and that of others. This doesn't mean that they bend over backwards to give everyone exactly what they want when they want it, but it does mean that they seek compromise when it is expedient. When there is no room for flexibility, they know how to communicate expectations in a language that doesn't feel like an order coming down from on high.

Perhaps most importantly, they do all of this because they care. They don't do it just for the sake of doing it or out of some sense of duty. They genuinely care. Their compassion runs through their every fiber. The servant leaders shows his or her team in both word and deed that they have value and are entitled to dignity. This is how they show them they understand. It's how they prove and apply their emotional intelligence.

8

The Optics of Leadership—The Seen and the Unseen

"God does not see as a mortal, who sees the appearance.
The Lord looks into the heart."

—1 Samuel 16:7

Perceptions are important. If we are perceived as untrustworthy or inauthentic, we'll never be able to lead a culture change. We might want to be servant leaders, but we'll never be able to get there without the right optics. While optics aren't everything, they are an important part of leadership. How others perceive us as leaders will either help or hinder our ability to lead them effectively.

Few people are scrutinized in the way that leaders are. Everything we do or say is put under the microscope, and, without the context of the larger picture, our words and actions might seem insensitive or even cruel (indeed, they might *be* insensitive or cruel), even when this was not our intention.

We cannot entirely control how we are perceived, but we can do more to mitigate the likelihood of misperceptions. This starts and ends with communication. I often work toward this when conducting workshop around temperament models, communication, teambuilding, and conflict navigation. So much of the issues we face in our personal and professional lives stem from the same root: ineffective communication.

Each of us receives information filtered through various lenses—through our temperaments, our experiences, and our biases. These lenses shape, shade and sometimes even completely change what we're hearing. Ineffective communicators plow straight ahead without stopping to consider how their messages are being received. Servant leaders seek to understand what kind of messages can pass intact through all different shapes and thicknesses of lenses.

What is Said and Unsaid

When you're having trouble getting your message across (when it's being perceived in ways other than you intended), you'll find yourself constantly repeating yourself. Work often has to be redone, and when it gets done, outcomes will be less than expected. These are all symptoms of communication problems that almost always start at the top (and just as often are blamed on those at the bottom).

More often than not, though, the problem is not rooted in what we say. It's something deeper. In his landmark 1971 book, *Silent Messages*, Albert Mehrabian argued that what we say is *far* less important than how we say it. Mehrabian says that only 7% of our communication credibility is based on what we say; 55% of how we are perceived is based on our body language, and 38% is based on the tone of our voice. Saying the right thing at the right time is important, but we need to pay very close attention to how our physical presence speaks its own language.

Mannerisms and posture can strengthen our communication, or (when they send mixed signals) they can weaken it dramatically. For instance, I have been accused on more than one occasion of having RBF (resting b**** face). When I am deep in thought or intently listening, I lift my chin and tilt my head a bit to hear better out of my right ear. When I'm close to understanding something (but not quite there), I'll purse my lips into a pucker, furrow my eyebrows, and twitch my lips from left to right. These signals are sometimes misinterpreted, so I sometimes have to remind myself to smile or to nod along to show them I'm engaged and interested.

It is my responsibility to be aware of what my body is saying—to understand the layers of language that I speak with my body both when I'm speaking and when I'm silent. I need to understand how I can be and have been misinterpreted. Armed with this understanding, I can begin cutting these misunderstandings off either before they occur or, at the very least, while they are occurring.

Treat All the Same by Treating All Differently

Ultimately, people want the same things. They want to do a good job, and they want their hard work to be appreciated and acknowledged in ways that resonate deeply within them. We need to do our best to make sure we are addressing this need for all those we lead. Paradoxically, this means we need to treat all the same by treating all differently.

This means we need to lead (whenever possible) in ways that show we have at least considered the mixtures of temperaments, strengths, and circumstances that make the members of our team unique. This might sound like pie-in-the-sky nonsense, so let me explain my meaning.

Let's assume two employees (we'll call them John and Jane) with roughly equal abilities. By some measures of fairness, we should treat John the same way we treat Jane, but this isn't what servant leaders do. They make adjustments, big or small, depending on the person.

Let's say that John and Jane have both been inconsistent in terms of meeting expectations. They're both spending too much time socializing with other staff members, which is not only interfering with their own productivity, it is also interfering with the abilities of others to do what they need to do.

Now, let's look a little deeper. John is an extremely social person. He cares deeply about his coworkers. Jane is more closed off. She is usually a by-the-book employee, but she's been emerging from her shell in the past few months. Still, she remains a process-driven employee.

Though the issue is essentially the same, an effective approach with John will be one that focuses on his socializing as a disruption. It's impacting the members of his team. By pulling their attention away from their tasks, he is creating problems *for them.* He is letting them down.

For Jane, an effective approach will be more formal. While she would surely understand a conversation that focused on how she is impacting her team members, this won't resonate as deeply with her. She cares about her coworkers, but telling her that she is creating problems for them won't be as effectual as a focus on the systems and the overall process that she's disrupting with her inconsistency.

Both have a desire to succeed, so it's simply a matter of painting a slightly different picture for each of them of what success will look like. When we adjust this picture so that the light captures different elements, leaving others in the shadow, we can capture the viewer's attention. They'll connect with and understand the picture we're showing them at a glance.

Let Them See You—Good or Bad

People look to their leaders as a source of calm when the horizons darken. When rising winds begin shaking the timbers and the waves threaten the ship and all those on board, your crew will look to you. If they see cracks in your courage, they'll start running for the lifeboats as fast as their legs will carry them.

> **"Courage [is] not the absence of fear, but the triumph over it. The brave man is not he who does not feel afraid, but he who conquers that fear."**
>
> — Nelson Mandela

We must build up our resiliency. This is a continual and communal process. Resilient leaders, by remaining pliant and calm in moments of crisis, build cultures of resilience. Their teams rally around them in difficult times. Those you lead will know that they can put their faith in you, know that you can and will restore and replenish what has been damaged or diminished. It's a matter of giving them something to believe in. They need to see a vision of you at your absolute best. This will be the touchstone for their faith.

This is never more important than when the pressure rises. My mother was a nurse for 45 years. Although the ability to remain calm under pressure is in the nursing job description, my mother had this quality in spades. She was the calm port in the storm that both patients and colleagues could rely on.

She raised six children while caring (without a word of complaint) for her elderly mother-in-law. It seemed that, no matter what the crisis, she was always bigger than the problem. When I was quite young, my older brother was in a motorcycle accident in front of our house. His injuries were extensive, and I can remember watching my mother calmly giving directives to the rest of the family while she climbed into the back of the ambulance. When the pressure rose, her nursing instincts took over.

For a long time, I wondered whether I had this same set of instincts. As a young girl, the sight of blood would make me squeamish. My mother wore a starched white nurse's uniform (complete with white shoes, stockings, and, of course, the iconic white cap), and she would frequently come home from work with blood on her clothes—sometimes a lot of it. The first thing she would do is soak her uniform in a bucket of cold water so the blood wouldn't set in.

It was my job to put her uniform in the wash after it'd been soaking for a while, and this meant I had to put my hands in that bloody water. I hated this chore. It made my skin crawl and my stomach churn every time. My sisters teased me for my squeamishness. Nursing was in their blood, but it clearly wasn't in mine. I knew I was destined to do something else.

However, this isn't to say that I didn't have "nursing instincts". I may have convinced myself that I didn't have them, but when the pressure rose, I found myself, like my mom and my sisters, rising to meet the moment.

When I was a teenager in the mid-eighties, we lived in the country. There wasn't a movie theater or a bowling alley anywhere to be found so we had to find our own entertainment. We would ride our bikes around in the evenings until it started to get dark. On our rides, we'd seldom see anyone else (only a handful of cars drove on those roads). One evening, my brother had been riding his bike with a few friends, and a game of one-upmanship had taken a dangerous turn. Marcus tried to jump his ten-speed bike over a pile of rocks, and the result had been boy and bike piled together on the asphalt.

He rode his bike home and went straight into the bathroom. A few minutes later, he emerged with a bloody washcloth covering half of his face.

"What happened?" I asked.

"Nothing, I fell off my bike."

"Let me see," I said, bringing my hand to his face. He let me remove the washcloth. His cheek was bloody pulp. I could see his exposed cheekbone.

I felt a wave of nausea rush over me, but I pushed through it. Mom was working the night shift that night, so I knew I couldn't panic. She had shown me what resilience looks like; in that moment, I filled her white shoes.

I directed my brother to the truck, telling my dad that Marcus would need stitches and I would drive him to the hospital emergency room and for him to stay at home with my youngest brother. Dad called to tell Mom what had happened and that we were on our way to the emergency room at the hospital where she was working.

I could feel the adrenaline flowing as I sped our way to the hospital. I focused on my breaths, doing my best to remain calm and keep my eyes focused on the road. I had the window wide open, and the cool night air on my face seemed to help. When we got to the hospital (in record time), my hands were stiff from the white-knuckle drive. The nurses arrived and took Marcus into a triage bay and pointed me in the direction of an empty seat in the waiting room.

Mom was working in the ICU, so the staff notified her when we arrived. Minutes later, she arrived, and we talked briefly and calmly about what had happened. She then disappeared through the double doors to the triage bay. She didn't come back for 45 minutes, but she came with good news. Marcus would be just fine, except for a few nice scars that would surely impress the girls at school.

The crisis had passed, and a sense of relief washed over me. I let go of the feelings I was holding inside and allowed the tears to flow. I didn't have to be strong anymore. I had remained in control, but now I could let myself be carried away by my emotions.

Though I didn't realize it at the time, I was training myself for leadership. I was training my mind how to respond in moments of crisis. Like the nurses I grew up watching, business leaders are expected to assess quickly, triage, and address the most urgent needs to stabilize the situation and take action accordingly. Nurses receive years of training that prepare them for these moments. They lean on their instincts, but also on their training. The vast majority of business leaders, even if they have a good head for business, don't have the training they need to prepare them for these crises. They have to learn as they go.

If you're relatively new to leadership, you might find yourself feeling overwhelmed when dealing with your first real crisis. Remember, these are the chances to show yourself at your best. You're expected to remain calm, but don't get obsessed with never letting cracks show. People look to leaders during a crisis for reassurance, but they also want to see that you're human. This doesn't mean that you crumble when the stress mounts—merely that the members of your team see that it is only natural to react with some degree of emotion. If you appear cold or unfeeling, your team will feel as though they're up against it on their own. They won't feel as though they have an ally. They'll only see you as an overseer.

This is a balancing act. If you feel yourself tipping towards an over-emotional response, find a quiet space where you can be alone and use the square breathing technique (count to four on each as you inhale, hold, exhale and hold) to regain your balance. Count backwards from twenty, or give your overheating brain a simple task like identifying everything blue in the room. Your composure will soon return.

9

Universal Awareness

"Awareness is the greatest agent for change."

—Eckhart Tolle

Those who find themselves elevated to leadership positions often possess the ability to get *in the zone.* They can tune out distractions and focus on the task at hand. For years, I was one of these people. Without knowing it, though, this was creating a problem for me. As I grew better at detail-oriented thinking, I began to lose sight of the larger picture—of the broader context. I was marginally aware of myself and others, but I wasn't as aware of what was going on outside of my frame of reference.

As a cradle Catholic, I have often heard it said that ours is the "universal church." It wasn't until a few years ago that I learned the origins of the word *catholic.* It comes from the Greek word *katholikos,* meaning universal or all-encompassing. St. Ignatius of Antioch was the first to use this word in the context of the church in 110 AD. During his captivity, while being transported to Rome for execution, he wrote seven letters (epistles) to Christian congregations in the Mediterranean. In these epistles, he referred to these congregations collectively as the "Catholic" (universal) Church. St. Ignatius was describing a church that was unified, one in which all Christians came together as one body.

St. Ignatius desired to fuse the many into the one, and today, I hear in the word *catholic* more than just my denomination. I hear a call to bring people together under one roof, to find unity in diversity. We are not called to pave over differences but, rather, to create a place where all are welcome.

As we recognize the differences in others and learn to appreciate that these differences represent value added not subtracted, we can start to see why it is so crucial to build and encourage diversity into our teams and our organizations. This demands a policy of inclusion (a key component of universal awareness). A policy of inclusion brings in different strengths to complement one another. It is built on an understanding that the whole is greater than the sum of the parts.

We must understand that we are participants in a larger ecosystem. Our actions affect others within the ecosystem, rippling outwards to touch nearly every facet of the organization including our customers. The tasks you do are not just oriented in what you have going on right now in your own little piece of the organization. Everything affects everything else.

This first thing we need to ask ourselves is: *Where do the ripples go?*

Visualize the world as a pond with yourself at its center. Self-awareness means seeing how what we do affects our own emotional state. Social awareness means that we watch how the ripples spread outwards towards others. Universal awareness means being able to see how these ripples extend even beyond this. We know that they extend further than we can see, but we know they're there, moving ever outwards.

The further we can track these ripples, the broader our understanding grows. Armed with this broader understanding, we become better leaders because we are better equipped to solve much larger problems. When our focus is narrow, so too is our impact. By simply looking beyond the end of our noses and allowing ourselves to be exposed to things outside of our immediate orbit, we might start to get an idea of how much we've been missing.

While they are grounded in their beliefs and values, servant leaders remain open-minded. They are curious about other ways of doing things, about other cultures, about perspectives different from their own. Their critical thinking skills are an amalgamation of all they have learned and all they have seen. They don't know it all—far from it. If anything, they understand just how small they are and how large the pond is.

This concept might sound intimidating, so remember that we don't need to see it all. We just need to be aware that the ripples keep on going even when we can't see them. This isn't about omniscience. You don't need to know what DonNatalio in Madagascar had for lunch; you just need to understand that there is a broader world that feels and responds to our presence and our actions (broader than many of us realize).

Servant leaders may not have a universal perspective (this is more than mortals can hope for), but they show a universal awareness by *seeking* that broader understanding. When they encounter a problem, they look beyond just themselves for a solution. It might be something they've done that has worked before, but it just as well might be something that worked in the next office over, or it might be something that worked in Brazil or France. Everybody has something to teach us, and servant leaders are always open to new learnings.

Our Responsibility

This kind of awareness demands a tremendous amount of energy. It's not something that we can just allow to happen. Self-awareness demands that we open our eyes wide enough to see ourselves; social awareness demands that we open our eyes wider still so we can see others; universal awareness demands much more from us. Yes, we need to open ourselves, but we also need to actively seek information about areas in which we are making or might possibly make an impact. It's a much broader approach, and we can't approach it passively.

How does the servant leader do this? How does the servant leader balance all that their roles require and grow their awareness at the same time? How do they find the mental capacity required to pay attention to *all* of it?

The first thing we need to understand is that the leader's responsibility is not to micromanage everything. The leader's primary function is to lead and develop the people who are performing the tasks. You may need to have a basic understanding how the various roles you are overseeing fit into the larger plan, but you do not necessarily need to know how to perform each of the tasks. You *definitely* don't need to do it all yourself.

Servant leaders have, at some point or another, learned how to be effective at equipping and empowering others. Few things take more courage than to empower others in areas under your responsibility, but few things are more crucial when you want to start expanding your awareness and impact. Few things take up our time and energy like micromanagement. This might feel like the only way to get things done, but it's actually gumming up the works.

Become better at equipping and empowering others and you'll be one step closer to being a better leader.

Building our Universal Awareness

If universal awareness is something you want to develop, you'll need to get out from behind your desk and get involved! Find something you can be passionate about outside of just your work or primary areas of responsibilities. Do something different!

Look for organizations in your area where you can meet people from all walks of life. Common interests will help connections develop quickly, but different perspectives will turn those connections into opportunities to grow your awareness. Look for experiences and opportunities that may not necessarily tie into your specific work or industry. Contribute to your community by serving in a homeless shelter, support the

United Way or other charitable organizations, do meaningful community-serving work.

Professional networking groups can also be a great place to start. Before you dive in, though, take a moment to consider what you want to gain from these groups. If you want your awareness to be industry-specific, you may want to begin with a professional association for your field of work or industry. If you are looking to expand your awareness on a broader scale, take a look at other organizations that may offer a more diverse membership like Rotary clubs, Business Networking International, or your local Chamber of Commerce.

If there is nothing available in your area that appeals to you, perhaps this is your chance to create a networking group from scratch. Take some time to identify what it is you are looking for. What types of people do you want to connect with? What are the demographics? What age groups, professional backgrounds, and levels of industry expertise are you interested in? What are your objectives? Are you looking for referrals, or do you want to share knowledge and collaborate on passion projects?

Once you have a vision of what an ideal network would look like, put out some feelers. You may be surprised by how many people respond. What you'll soon see is that there are other people on a journey similar to yours. This is what universal awareness opens our eyes to. Yes, we see a world of difference, but we also see how, deep down, we're all looking for similar things.

10

Know Thyself and Know Thy People

"He who knows others is wise; he who knows himself is enlightened."

—Lao Tzu

When we are growing our understanding, it's important to have a focus point. We may want a 360-degree understanding, but we can only get this a few degrees at a time. We get it by bringing our focus to ourselves and to the people we are leading.

Especially if you have been recently promoted into a leadership position, the work of assessing the strengths and weaknesses of your team (including yourself) is absolutely crucial. We can't rely on assumptions, and we can't lean on the assessments of our predecessors. We need to do this work ourselves. We must build our understanding from scratch. This work allows you to begin laying that foundation of trust. This trust moves in both directions. When you know yourself and your people, you'll know you can trust them, and they'll know they can trust you.

Know Thyself

Most leadership coaches utilize some sort of assessment tool very early in the coaching process. To form a leader, we coaches must first understand who they are and why they make leadership decisions the way that they do. If you want to become a better leader (ideally, to become a servant leader) you have two options in front of you for that assessment:

1) You can do the assessment yourself.
2) You can have a professional leadership coach facilitate an assessment for you.

Self-assessment is more difficult, but many people find it an intensely rewarding journey. My experience has been that professionally guided assessments return deeper insights than self-guided ones. We take it for granted that we understand ourselves and our motivations, but it's often the case that, when someone starts digging a little, what we uncover is surprising.

One of my clients and I were talking about how his team perceives him, and he kept circling back to the same two words: *not lazy*. Over the course of 20 minutes or so, he used these exact words four or five times. I stopped him and asked him about his choice of words. He seemed genuinely surprised, and when I asked him why it was important to him that others see him as the hardest worker in the office, I could see him struggling to hold back a realization.

He was your textbook definition of a workaholic, and this seemed to stem from an insecurity about how he was being perceived. As a leader, he felt it was his duty to work harder than everyone else. He couldn't risk being perceived as lazy, so he piled more and more on his plate, giving himself very little time for rest and recuperation.

He needed to have this pointed out to him. He couldn't see it himself, and this is true for each of us. We are often blind to our own hang-ups and insecurities. He had to be told that he could occasionally let his foot off the gas, and this is exactly what he did. He found a more sustainable and reasonable work/life priority balance, and now he's happier for it. He's found that sweet spot where professional performance and personal satisfaction dovetail, and it started with this single moment of insight.

A professional leadership coach worth their salt has experience getting to the root of leadership issues. They'll be able to ask you those questions that will result in those *aha* moments. Guiding yourself to these questions is possible, but it takes an extremely high level of self-awareness.

Whether you get to know yourself on your own or with the help of a professional, this knowledge has the power to utterly transform your leadership abilities. When we know what our triggers are and *why* they drive us to do what we do and react as we react, we can stop being the problem. We can start solving problems rather than creating them. We won't be perfect—far from it—but we will be able to recognize when our imperfections are blurring or distorting things.

This is why we seek to know ourselves—so that we can get out of our own way and out of the way of those we lead.

Know Thy People

You can't lead someone effectively if you don't understand them. A lot of managers who want to institute a culture change or lift performance start with employee surveys, but I've never found these to be all that effective in these situations. I've seen it all too often. Even if they turn up something productive, they are prone to backfiring. They begin with the best of intentions, but they release a backdraft of complaints and negativity that can be extremely difficult to get back under control.

As tempting as it might be to blame employees for inaccurate or unclear results, this is rarely where the fault lies. A lack of responses or (even worse) responses from only a few disgruntled staff can severely skew the results of your survey. This can have more to do with how the survey was administered than how employees actually handled it.

Surveys are often mishandled from start to finish. Questions are either too precise or too broad to be meaningful, communication surrounding the survey and how it will be used is vague, and managers sit on the results for too long (long enough to convince those who participated in the survey that the whole thing was a waste of effort).

In the worst examples, management shares the survey results, focusing on the positive and glossing over the negative responses. When employees take a risk and elevate a problem, they expect some response. If you ignore the issues they raise, this comes off as cowardly. You're effectively telling them that they are braver than the organization they work for—never a good signal.

Before I left the healthcare industry, I was asked to take the reins in a number of struggling agencies. I adopted a different approach than my predecessors, and that difference made all the difference. The first thing I did seemed obvious to me (but apparently not obvious to everyone else). I would start by meeting individually with as many people as I could. I saw each meeting as a new opportunity to get to know the people as people. This meant going beyond their job description and work history (information that was available in their HR file). I needed to go deeper, to get a feel for them as individuals.

I would schedule full days of 30-minute meetings, starting with key people and radiating outwards from there. I would ask them what they felt they contributed to the team and what they felt their strengths were, but these questions were just the entrée. For the main course, I served up questions that probed deeper. I would ask them about their strengths and weaknesses (not just in their role, but in a broader sense). I would ask them what they enjoyed doing, what their goals were, and how they wanted to grow. When they told me about career aspirations, I would ask them what they were willing to do to make these goals tangible. What wouldn't they do? Where would they draw their line in the sand? What were their biggest personal priorities? What would they do if they were the ones making the decisions?

These meetings weren't interrogations. They were conversations, with the answer to one question informing the conversation's direction. Sometimes we'd get through quite a few questions; other times we would spend the entire meeting talking about their underutilized skills, their career aspirations, or their growth potential.

These meetings set the tone for the relationship that would follow. It showed them what they could expect from me, and it gave them a chance to tell me, in their own words, what I could expect from them. They understood my position, and I understood theirs. I saw the agency's problems from their perspective, and this made it easier to determine how they might fit into the solution.

Remember, changes in leadership create anxiety in the team. There is uncertainty and fear. They don't know what to expect, so you need to put their minds at ease by making a connection with them and showing them what kind of leader you'll be. I found that, by starting a conversation and quickly making the conversation personal, I was able to quell their fears and bring down the barriers that separate the leaders from the led.

We started the relationship on the right foot. They were connecting with me and I was connecting with them.

Who is on Your Bus?

In *Good to Great,* Jim Collins says that, when we're building teams, we can think about it like seating people on a bus. As the driver of the bus, it's your job, first of all, to make sure you know who is on the bus (i.e., to know your people). Once you know who is on the bus, you can start looking at what seats they are in. Is everybody sitting in the right place? Is there anybody on the bus who might be sitting in the wrong place? Is there anybody who is clearly on the wrong bus? Are there people waiting at the next stop who might fill some of the empty seats?

In 2010, I was tasked with turning around a couple of struggling homecare agencies. If we stick with the bus metaphor, we can say that their bus was going nowhere fast. The driver was blind and deaf, and all the passengers were facing in different directions. The wheels had come off. It was a wreck waiting to happen.

The team had been through five directors in four years, so they had no faith in me. I was, to them, just another new face—soon to be a distant memory. While I was still warming the seat, two key staff members, Stephanie and Lana, walked into my office and informed me that they would both be getting off at the next stop.

I asked them to commit to two more weeks. They said they could do that. I then asked them for one further commitment. I asked them to swap seats. For the first week, each would train the other; for the second week, they would give it the old college try in their new roles. "If you still want to leave," I said, "I'll accept your resignation with no hard feelings and wish you well."

It didn't even take two weeks. After the first week, they both decided to stay. The role change had been a breath of fresh air for both of them, but it wasn't just the change they needed. Lana was highly structured in her approach to everything; a role in scheduling made what had once been a limitation a strength. Stephanie was highly extroverted, which allowed her to excel in a more customer service-oriented role that saw her speaking with new people almost every single day.

They both felt like they would be able to make a significant contribution to the organization in their new roles, and they ended each day with a sense of accomplishment. They were no longer merely punching the clock. They were happy with the seats they had on the bus. The organization had the right butts in the right seats.

Between the Lines

When I asked Stephanie and Lana to switch seats, I was confident that my gambit would work. I'd never tried something similar, but, in a way, they had told me it would work. They had both been assigned tasks they were only partially suited to. There was no natural fit between their natural abilities and their roles, and this meant that, even when they were successful, they were never completely satisfied.

When we were able to align their skills and their roles, we were able to boost their confidence, performance, and job satisfaction. They were happier with their seats on the bus, and the organization saw and treated them as valued members of the team. When I left the organization, they were still excelling in their respective roles.

Remember, God made us with two ears and one mouth for a reason. We should be listening at least twice as much as we are speaking. This comes, for many, with a considerable degree of discomfort. There's a feeling—especially among those new to leadership roles—that every silence needs to be filled with either a question or an instruction. When you lean into that silence, though, you will be surprised by how much people reveal. Even a few seconds of silence can prove revelatory—provided that it's clear that the onus is on them to break the silence.

We want to give our people time and space to tell their stories. They're in the trenches day after day, so they probably know more about what is going on down there than you do. You may have been in the trenches yourself (perhaps even recently), but don't assume that their story is the same as yours. Let them describe problems from their perspective. Listen, take notes, and listen some more. Ask them how things look from where they're sitting. Ask them to help you understand anything that isn't immediately transparent.

The solution is there—between the lines of their story.

Knowing Begins Where Assumptions End

I once wanted to acknowledge an employee for going above and beyond. Without complaint, she had taken on a boatload of extra responsibilities when one of her coworkers went on leave. She had been working long hours, and I was sure that she was going home exhausted at the end of each day.

The coworker returned and things went back to normal, but I didn't want to let her extra work go unrecognized. As a little token of my appreciation, I gave her a gift card for a deluxe pedicure at a local spa. Pedicures are one of my favorite ways to treat myself when the pressure mounts, and I assumed that she would enjoy the pampering. Who doesn't like a good pedicure, right? Wrong.

If I'd only asked her what she wanted (rather than making assumptions), I'd have seen how wrong I was. She had two small children at home, and finding childcare was a daily challenge for her. What I thought would be a nice break was, from her perspective, a burden.

What's worse, she was borderline phobic about her feet. When I gave her the gift certificate, it was clear that I had struck a wrong chord. She told me that the thought of someone else touching and rubbing her feet made her skin crawl. I couldn't have picked a worse way to recognize her if I had tried.

I told her that I wanted to recognize her contribution and asked her how I could do that in a way that would make her happy. All she wanted, she said, was a bit of time off (with pay) so she could catch up on some of the time she had spent away from her children. We arranged this, and she felt more-than-adequately compensated for the extra effort she had put in.

I was glad that she spoke frankly with me about the gift. It reminded me that knowing begins where assumptions end. When we make assumptions, we are filling our knowledge gaps with our biases. Biases aren't *always* wrong. Acting on our assumptions might work in our favor, but it's a gamble that we don't need to make. When we seek understanding by asking questions and listening carefully to the answers, we can develop a more accurate picture of the people we lead. With this more accurate picture, when we act in ways that we think are in their best interest, we will, more times than not, hit the mark.

Assumptions can be costly, both for us and for the organizations we lead. They can cost us business, good will, and (what may never be regained) credibility. The more often we lean on assumptions, the more likely it becomes that we will make that unpardonable mistake.

Leaders who frequently make assumptions quickly develop a reputation for being unreasonable. They leap to conclusions without checking the facts. One of my clients was having issues with staff not properly ordering inventory, which was causing significant delays. She repeated the same instructions over and over, assuming that her staff were either misunderstanding her or just being lazy. She never challenged her assumptions or even asked her staff what the problem was.

When we investigated it together, it turned out that there was a missing link in the communication chain. Rather than working off the concrete data, they had to make assumptions about when product supplies would run low. These assumptions (like their manager's) consistently missed the mark by a wide margin. We solved the problem with a shelf quantity marker, and everybody learned something about what happens when we make assumptions.

Dictators never see their assumptions clearly. They believe they're always right—about everything. Servant leaders are *more often* right because they are wise enough to seek clarity before coming to a conclusion. They look before they leap.

Know Something? Do Something!

Few things damage leadership credibility faster and more permanently than deep dives into your personnel with absolutely no follow up. If you've asked for feedback, your team needs to see that their honesty hasn't been for nothing. They've given you feedback (both positive and negative), and they expect you to do something with it. They expect to see sustainable improvements in their chief areas of concern, and they'll want to see more of what they feel are the positives.

In one of the healthcare organizations I worked with recently, a considerable amount of feedback that came back to the organization surrounded the company's approach to paid holidays, particularly around festival season. In South Louisiana, Mardi Gras is equal parts celebration and disruption. Roads are closed for parades, making the commute a labyrinthine affair.

The result is a huge spike in the number of employees who request the day off, with some suggesting that, since the disruptions are out of their control, the organization should treat the day of the Mardi Gras parades as a paid holiday. So many people brought this up during our organizational reviews that it was clear something had to be done.

The organization wasn't willing to accept the losses that would come with paying all of its employees to stay home for the day, but there was a widespread interest in giving employees an option. It was decided that each employee would be given a choice: they could take *either* Mardi Gras or Memorial Day as a paid day off. The office would run on a skeleton staff on both days.

The solution was a satisfying compromise. Employees had more flexibility, and the bottom-line impact for the organization would be marginal. Most importantly, it ensured that patient care wouldn't be interrupted. In any other industry, it might have been reasonable to expect the organization to close the office on both days, but, as my mother would say, "People don't stop getting sick or needing care just because it's a holiday."

Servant leaders don't just provide an opportunity for people to express their grievances or concerns; they listen carefully when their people speak up and respond appropriately, trying (whenever possible) to balance the interests of the organization and the needs of its people.

Allow time and space for your team members to approach you with questions or concerns. Servant leaders spend considerable time and resources on making sure that changes, even when unwelcome, are understood and rationalized. You can't please all the people all the time, but you can make sure that everyone feels heard.

11

Building Awareness into Your Teams

"Leadership is unlocking other people's potential to become better."

—Bill Bradley

Servant leaders don't just change how they think. They change the thinking patterns of those around them. Their self-awareness is infectious. Even if we are growing as individuals and leaders, we cannot say we are growing as servant leaders if we're leaving our people behind. We need to take them with us, helping them grow.

Self-aware teams are more likely to put in that necessary effort—more likely to go beyond the bare minimum when called upon. When we start to understand how ramifications can ripple outwards, we're far less likely to be careless or insensitive. When we see how broad our impact truly is, we can start to take responsibility for what we do and how we do it. Without that knowledge, it's easy to shrug off the unseen consequences.

Team members who lack self-awareness often create tension in their relationships (both vertical and lateral), and this tension can often be released when we help them see themselves through new eyes. More often than not, the building tension is the result of a lack of direct communication. They might have received warnings or even discipline surrounding specific behaviors, but the underlying causes of these behaviors remain unaddressed. These are, to be sure, uncomfortable conversations, and nobody wants to be the first to say something, but this burden falls squarely on our shoulders.

I was once helping repair team dynamics in a healthcare organization, and there was one manager who nearly everyone identified as a problem when asked privately. Her communication style was abrasive and condescending, and she seemed unable to inspire her team to excel in any way. Issues had been raised with her, but always on the superficial level. Her superiors had asked her to address specific problematic behaviors, but she'd never been asked to address the mindset that was producing these behaviors.

We brought the matter forward, and we pushed her to examine the underlying causes of her abrasive leadership style. You could see the cracks forming almost immediately (I recognized this look—the same look I must have worn when I was informed that my team thought I was cruel and cold). The conversation was a difficult one for everyone, but it was an eye-opening moment for the manager.

She had been convinced that her leadership style was not only expedient but necessary. Like so many leaders, she had absorbed messages about leaders being tough and inflexible, and she'd never stopped to think how it was affecting those she was managing. We talked for an hour or so later in the day, and she told me that she was insecure about how she was being perceived. She didn't have any post-secondary education or any formal leadership training. She had been thrown to the lions without sword or shield, and she was doing all she could with her teeth and nails. She didn't know any better. It was a familiar story.

As we talked, her self-awareness grew. She began to see her style in a different light. She began to see herself through her team's eyes, and this transformed her perspective. She didn't become a perfect leader overnight. It was a long journey for her, but seeing herself through new eyes was that all-important first step.

Preventative Maintenance

So where do you start? Think about it this way: Most new cars come with two user manuals. You've got the in-depth guide with all the fine print, but you've also got the quick start guide. When you encounter a problem, the first place you go is to the quick start guide. If you still can't find what you're looking for there, you dive deeper into the more detailed instructions.

Think of the general information that you have about your employee as your quick start guide. You have their resume, their human resources file, and there are probably extensive notes from initial interviews and on-boarding. These will get you started. These should tell you something about their existing level of self-awareness. If it is already high, all you'll have to do is put a little air in the tires. If self-awareness is a larger issue, you'll probably need to pop the hood and start taking a closer look at the problem areas.

The problem is that you don't really have the more detailed manual yet. This will only come as you explore the individual. Deeper and more concentrated conversations will start to help you fill in some of the details. They'll help you find that trigger (perhaps positive, perhaps negative) that will guide them towards self-awareness.

Remember that, even when we're dealing with a young new employee (perhaps in their first professional role), we're not buying a new car. We're buying a used one. It's got a history. To build self-awareness with them, we need to know that history. We need to know what their maintenance history is, and we need to know about the accidents too. Our initial assessment might turn up some of the things we'll need to work on, but it's just as likely that we won't discover the deeper issues until later.

How much later depends on how often we bring them into the shop for maintenance or repairs. If we wait until the car is on fire to pop the hood, we've let things go past the point of no return. If, however, we open that hood early—before performance issues become blatantly obvious—we can start to build self-awareness while the engine is still getting hot. We can build it into their growth as a member of the team.

Doing this work early will mean fewer breakdowns. You'll still have to do regular maintenance, and you'll still need to top off the tank regularly with fuel. This means supporting and connecting with them, rewarding them for their efforts, and recognizing them for their contribution and growth. If they carry a heavy load, you'll need to refuel them more frequently than those who are merely supporting members of the fleet.

If you can't get to the root of the problem on your own, rather than sending the car straight to the junkyard, call a mechanic. The solution that is eluding you might be simpler than you think. Sometimes a trained professional can ask the right question or put the matter in the right light in just the right moment. If you're struggling to find that way to create self-awareness (either in a particular team member or across your entire team), a trained professional might be just the ticket.

Of course, there may come a time when a car is just not a good fit. It can't carry your growing family, or its performance issues have made anything more than short trips to the store unmanageable. When the problems are this large, it's time to put something different in the garage. There are some challenges that neither maintenance nor the mechanic can fix. Servant leadership is about doing all we can, but there are limits to this. We can only help people to grow who want to grow, and we cannot force someone to fit into a space they simply are not equipped for.

Building Awareness Through Tough Questions and Team Building

When we are dealing with our team members one on one, we can help them raise their awareness by asking questions and redirecting their focus so that they can see and understand the larger picture.

We might feel like we are on the right track if we're helping them see the problem from two perspectives (ours and theirs), but these aren't the only perspectives to consider. There are often overlapping perspectives that need to be taken into account. Servant leaders have learned at some point or another how to see issues from multiple angles, and this isn't all. They're also adept at helping team members reach a similar level of awareness.

We can do this with some tough questions that will, if we give them time to think about it, broaden their perspective:

- What do you know to be true? How do you know it to be true?
- What are you taking for granted?
- Who have you chosen to believe? Why?
- Who might be impacted by this? Who else have you not considered?
- What might these impacts look like? How do these impacts help explain some of the resistance you've been getting?
- What else could you have done?
- How would a different path have affected the outcome?
- What do you think he/she is feeling right now?
- How do you want them to feel about this? How is this realistic?

When we are working with our teams as a whole, we can achieve something similar with team building and communication exercises that will help team members start to recognize that their perspective isn't the only one worth considering.

You can't leave this up to chance by simply throwing them into a room together for an unstructured gripe session. They're more likely to come out of these meetings grumbling than holding hands and singing Kumbaya. Give team building the attention and resources it deserves. Bring in a facilitator or moderator to ensure there are healthy exchanges and that you are getting the most out of that time together.

During these sessions, growth often happens in parallel. While the individual is learning to be more self-aware, they are also learning to be more socially aware. They are watching their teammates learn and grow, and this challenges them to do the same.

When there is a facilitator (which there should be, especially if you're leading a large team), they play the part of neutral party. They bring a disinterested perspective into the group and help bring new eyes to long-standing issues.

Perhaps most importantly, the facilitator creates a safe space for team members to discuss issues openly without fear of reprisals. It's difficult to overstate the importance of this. Although so much of the necessary servant leader work takes place on our own, our relationship with our teams and their relationships with each other are burdened with histories. These histories often make it difficult to see the truth—even when it is painfully obvious.

I've found that team building like this brings with it a host of benefits:

- Increased collaboration
- More effective communication
- Increased engagement
- Reduced resistance
- Fewer issues requiring management intervention

According to a recent Salesforce report, 86% of employees and executives cite either a lack of collaboration or ineffective communication for workplace failures. The same report found that well over half of employees cited strong team dynamics as reason to stay with an organization (longer even than was in their best interest), with two thirds of these saying that these dynamics were the primary reason for their remaining with the organization.

If you can bring your teams together, this will give you the time and space you need to address some of the other issues. You'll be able to move forward—each serving each other.

As a servant leader, you should be tasking yourself with bringing your teams closer together. Encourage their growth by sending them (either alone or together) to educational experiences in places where they'll be exposed to new people and new perspectives.

Expose your team members to the needs of the community by signing your organization up for a charitable cause that will demand some form (even a small one) of participation from all of you. Donating to a good cause is a good start, but it rarely broadens perspectives and brings teams together like joining forces and serving the community as a unified group.

As we learn to serve our teams, we are teaching them to be servants themselves. You'll know it's working when you see them becoming more eager to serve others. This is the ultimate goal of servant leadership: first to discover the servant leader within ourselves, and then to help others do the same.

Conclusion: The Power of Influence

As we start to change our leadership style to align ourselves with a servant position, we'll start to feel our influence grow. As we start to lead with a servant's heart, we'll be inspiring love, and this too brings influence with it. We have to be mindful, though. With this influence comes a tremendous responsibility—a responsibility to lead others ethically. True servant leaders lead their people and their organizations to *better* places, not just more profitable ones.

The important question is not (or should not be) *Am I influential?* It should be *How and why am I influencing others?* To what end? *Quo Vadis*? Where are you going?

History is full of influential figures. Tyrants and autocrats have less often seized power with force than they have ridden waves of popular support to positions of power. They moved crowds, started movements, and gathered followers. They were able to convince millions that they had the *only* solution to their problems, and they needed unlimited authority to make good on their promises. The people grant them that power, and only much later does it become apparent that, all along, this power was the goal. They used influence as a tool to help them get it.

At the same time, there are others who see their influence as a responsibility. Take Mother Teresa as an example. In Gallup polls, she was voted one of the ten most influential women in the world 18 times over the course of her lifetime. She used that influence to direct the world's attention to the poorest of the poor. She unified people around humanitarian challenges that might never have been noticed without her pointing them out. She made the world a better place with her own actions, but just as importantly, she moved others towards an identical servant position. She made the world better by being better, but also by showing others how to be better.

Servant leaders can do the same. You'll know when you're getting it right. You'll feel it deep down. You'll feel others getting better around you, and you'll know that at least some of this change is the result of your influence. Remember (as Mother Teresa remembered) that influence is a gift but also a responsibility. Use yours wisely, lovingly, and selflessly.

You'll feel yourself changing. When I discovered the servant leader within, it allowed me to let go. I had spent decades attempting to control both myself and those around me. With servant leadership, I became better in every way. Rather than obsessing about others' perceptions of me, I could turn my attention to helping others grow. I found empowerment by empowering others.

As an empowered and empowering leader, my life became much less stressful and much more fulfilling. I could feel myself growing, and I saw new possibilities for growth—new ways I could grow and use my influence. When I was only focused on myself, my growth potential was profoundly limited. When

I started to help others grow, that potential exploded outwards in every direction.

When you discover the servant leader within, you'll soon understand exactly what this means. You'll see that, when you step out from behind the curtain and lead honestly, courageously, and selflessly, your impact will be limitless.

Acknowledgements

There are a number of people who deserve to be acknowledged for all they have done to make my work and this book possible. First, I want to thank my children, Kassie, Kevin and Karson, who, in spite of some less-than-perfect parenting, have grown into remarkably strong and resilient young adults. I am inspired by each of you every day, and I love you more than you could ever know.

Thank you to Kassie for being the first one on the team and my number one supporter of this leadership journey I am on. I continue to be inspired by your wisdom beyond your years.

Thank you to Kevin and your true servant's heart. Every time I've volunteered your help, you've thrown yourself into it wholeheartedly. Know that you bless all those you encounter. A true gentleman, you are a living example of the spirit of modern chivalry. You give the best hugs, and it's impossible to frown when looking into your smiling eyes.

To Karson, thank you for keeping me humble and for keeping me on my toes. You have been a significant catalyst of God's work in directing our path. I know He has great things in store for you, and I'm blessed to be able to witness your life's journey.

Thank you to my dad, Malcolm, who showed me how love can help us find the strength we need to overcome even life's most challenging battles.

To my mom, Mary Ann, thanks for passing down your nursing DNA and your strength in faith. You were the first example for me of what true servant leadership looks like. I love and respect you so much.

Thank you to my sisters, Melissa "Lisa" and Melinda, for your continued influence in my life with your unique styles of nursing DNA. Thank you to my brothers, Mitchell, Marcus, and Micah, for your inspiring examples of resilience. I am the person I am today in part because of your collective influence. I love you all dearly.

Thank you to the friends and fellow leaders who willingly gave of yourself and your time to help me get unstuck at times during this process: Kristi Fredieu, Benjamin Dimas, Carmen Sims, Agnes Broussard, Molly Daigle, Bobby Fruge, Dr. Ryan Cazares, Mechelle Roberthon, Lyn Askin, and Kayla Stansbury. You like-minded leaders inspire and encourage my vision.

To Michael Norris, thanks for being the catalyst to spark radical movement in my spiritual journey. I will forever be grateful to God for placing you in my path during that season.

Thank you to the priests who have served and still serve as spiritual directors, advisors and inspirers: Fr. Jacob Dumont, LC, Fr. Michael Luxbacher, LC, Fr. Brice Higginbotham, Fr. Mark Toups, Fr. Jared Suire, and Fr. Alex Young, LC. Your guidance and assistance have been invaluable as I have developed the Servant's Table program.

To my editor, Bryan Szabo, thank you for being my collaborator and embarking together with me on one of the most challenging growth adventures of my life.

Heidi Melancon, Director of UL-SBDC for your continued guidance in navigating this entrepreneurial world.

Finally, to brandRUSSO, thank you for your generous support in bringing the images in my head to life.

About the Author

Monica Rougeau helps leaders who have a desire to grow. If you are feeling overwhelmed or stuck, Monica can help with leadership formation that will prepare you for next-level success.

In 2014, she stepped away from a successful corporate career and, soon after, she founded Elevare, which helps expedite leaders' growth through various modalities of leadership coaching and training.

She has successfully worked with entrepreneurs, senior executives, and emerging leaders in both the secular and the faith-based community, in the U.S. and abroad, bringing them from where they are to where they want to be.

Learn more about how Monica can help elevate you and your team to the next level at Elevareintl.com.

Made in the USA
Coppell, TX
02 August 2020

32310257R10085